READER REVIEWS

"Thank you so much for your wonderful book, your tribute, to the memory of Steve, Janette and Eliot. I felt honored to be included on the list of recipients of this truly unique memorial to your loved ones. All my memories of Steve center on his ability to light up a room by his presence, both as a kid and as an adult."
    Larry Titman
    Albuquerque, NM

"In my mind I have written you a hundred times since you dropped *I Alway Meant to Tell You* at my office.... I read the first few pages and couldn't go on until about a week ago.... Your book is a journey into self, a way of coming to closure.... We don't want to die with those words on our lips. We want to have told those we love how fully and wonderfully we love them."
    Dr. Teresa Balcomb
    Albuquerque, NM

"What a wonderful book! It was so much about you and Steve...the companions that make up our lives. Great work and indeed a significant effort and heartfelt."
    Jeff Burrows, Director
    Family Workshop, Albuquerque, NM
    Watermelon Mountain Jug Band (Co-founder)

"Thank you for writing the book. It has helped me so much.... I want you to know that as I closed the book, I brought it to my heart and just held it there while waves of love washed over me.... That is the true value of your book. It allows us to relive this time without keeping it always in our thoughts. That would be just too painful."
    Jeannie Purvines
    Albuquerque, NM

"An excellent account of one family's grieving for the sudden loss of three of its members—I found it personally very helpful for dealing with my own grief. Thank you."
    Marianne Greer
    Alberta, Canada

I Always Meant to Tell You...

I Always Meant to Tell You...

Letters to my little brother, Stephen Lloyd Wilkes (deceased)

Perry Robert Wilkes

Second Edition

Copyright 2003 Perry Robert Wilkes. All right reserved.

First Edition published in 2003 by Liberación Press and printed by Downtown Printing, Albuquerque, NM.

Second Edition, 2021, printed in the United States of America by IngramSpark for Liberación Press.

No part of this book may be used without written permission of the author, except in the case of brief quotations embodied in critical articles and reviews. For information, address the author at:
1912 Buffalo Dancer Trail NE
Albuquerque, NM 87112

Book and cover design by Carolyn Kinsman
Cover photograph courtesy Alice Rosenberger Wilkes Matvichuk

ISBN: 978-1-7350115-4-7

1. Grief and grieving 2. Family 3. Biography 4. Memoir

Preface to the Second Edition

Twenty years have passed since *I Always Meant to Tell You* was first published as a memorial to my brother Steve, his wife Dr Janette Carter, and their youngest son Eliot, after they perished in a plane crash in northern Alaska.

In those 20 years, the pain of the tragedy has never fully receded and I don't expect that it ever will. Their deaths still linger as a large gap in our family and nothing has happened, or could have happened, since then to fully bridge the chasm that was created.

We realize we are not the first family to have experienced such a tragedy, but now we must share that grief with many others who we may have not been able to relate to before we were also confronted with our own terrible pain. And we are now more fully aware of the precious gift that life bestows upon us. It's a dangerous world we live in. And as we reflect upon the probable number of times each of our ancestors narrowly missed being destroyed in some ancient war, tragic accident, or natural disaster, we must consider it a miracle that we are alive at all to share in this brief moment of our unique planet's long existence in a small and remote galaxy.

Although this book was written primarily for our family and for close friends who knew Steve's family well, many other people who have read the book have said that it has helped them through some of their own personal crises. This has been an unexpected result of its publication and I know that Steve, Janette, and Eliot would have been proud to hear that.

Recently our first printing company ceased producing books and we were faced with simply believing this book had served its original purpose and letting it go into history. But the response we've gotten over the years made us reconsider that idea.

And so it is an honor for us to republish *I Always Meant to Tell You* at this time. And we hope it remains a useful and timely resource for the reader.

Perry Robert Wilkes
Bahia de Kino, Sonora, MX
April, 2021

Dedication

This book is a very long letter to you, Stephen Lloyd Wilkes, my younger brother, my only brother, whom I knew for all of your 54 years, until you perished with most of your family on July 15, 2001 in the crash of a small plane near a quiet lake in northern Alaska. This is also a letter to your dear wife, Janette Carter, who died with you in that crash and who, I have just realized, I knew for maybe half her life. And it is a letter to your youngest son, Eliot, my wonderful nephew, only nine years old when he died that day along with his father and his mother.

This is a letter that has taken many months to write and which, truthfully, may never be finished. There is so much that I could say to all of you at this time, and which I feel that I should have said while you were still here among us. And now, while there seems to be some urgency on my part, as if maybe I can tell you these things in the few minutes before that small plane lifts into the sky for the last time, in truth, there is no longer any reason to hurry these thoughts. There is much yet to say. Far more than I can say to you in a few brief moments. There are things it will take me years to tell you. And now I am faced with an eternity in which I can attempt to do so.

And Steve, this is also a letter to Alec, your only surviving child, my oldest nephew.

There are many things, Alec, that you should know about your parents. You knew them well for all the years of your life as they nurtured your passage into young adulthood, and you have known things about your parents, those intimate family things which can never be known by others, that I can never be a party to. But there are things your parents said, and did, and felt, before you were born; and now there is no way for them to tell you of these things — to explain the choices they made in life, and tell you why. It is, I believe, one of the most important functions of our aunts, our uncles, our parents, and our grandparents, to tell us of our past, to fill in those gaps — those just forgotten and those purposefully neglected — in the lives of our loved ones. It is their duty to provide these stories as an explanation of our history, and as a forum for the discussion of meaning and intent in our actions.

In our family, this often occurred over a long game of Canasta on a Sunday evening after dinner. The card game itself is little more than an excuse for meaningful communion with one another. It doesn't even matter who wins the game. The cards are dealt, the rules are argued over — yet one more time — and during the evening, certain important moments are remembered, rediscussed, and recast into the endless tapestry that is a family's history. This imperfect history is more a joint memoir than a collection of dates, times, and verifiable events. Nobody will ever check the facts for veracity. The important thing here is the larger pattern of our family's life. And the process of family remembrance is an endless process; it begins anew each time the aunts gather with a youngster or two in the kitchen to prepare a meal, or whenever a couple of uncles sit on a porch swing to enjoy a sunset with one of the kids, or when the dishes are cleared from the table and a round of cards is dealt. That's when this ancient family ritual begins all over again. That's when the stories are told.

And this is the simple way in which our family insures that you will remember your past, Alec, and that you'll even get to know a few of those many people who were very old and who died when you were very young. And it's probably the only way you'll ever know those people who died long before you were born, and who you never could have met, but who are still a part of everything you do today and tomorrow and forever.

You're young now, Alec, and not much interested in these things, but you deserve to know the past before it's forgotten. It's your past, as remembered imperfectly by your family, and you should be made aware of the many successes, and yes, even the failures, of your family and your parents. They were not gods, but people. They were decent and honest and caring people who made their way through life as best they could. When they made a mistake they tried their best to learn from it, and not wallow in self-pity any more than may be necessary to repair the ego and mend the soul. I hope that the simple insights of your family in the many years that are to come will help you to form a balanced and realistic picture of those two remarkable individuals who were your parents, and of that cheerful young fellow who was your little brother.

This is a letter as well, to our three sisters, Elyse, Nancy, and Joan, their husbands Jimmy, Audón and Kevin, and all their children, my nieces and my nephews — Alec's aunts, uncles and cousins. And to our parents Alice and Perry, who have been divorced a very long time, and to Dad's wife Bette, and to Janette's mother, Rosalie. And it is a letter to our aunts, our uncles, our cousins, and to our friends, of which there are far too many to mention here.

This is a time for each of us to remember, and to tell the story of those times and events in the lives of three individuals who are forever memorable to you, and to each of us. There is much to be remembered, and there is time now in which to remember it. But it is important to do so, before memory fades and time escapes. So I'd also like to ask each of you to please take some little time from your life to put pen to paper, and record those events that remain meaningful to you in the lives of Steve, Janette, and Eliot.

At some time in the distant future these recorded moments will mean far more to the rest of us than you can now realize.

PRW
October, 2001
Bahia de Kino, Sonora

Acknowledgements

This is a book I never wanted to write.

I've been working on various writing projects for many years. But they were all suddenly pushed into the background by my brother's death, and I was faced by a daunting task.

Writing a book in memory of a remarkable individual like Stephen Lloyd Wilkes has been a difficult endeavor that required much thought. In occasional spare moments and in the annual solitude of a quiet Mexican village, thoughts began to take shape. Much of this remembrance is the result of conversations, cards and letters from friends and relatives. I thank them all for their insights and their kind words.

I appreciate the thoughts and words of our mother and father, Alice G. Rosenberger and Perry R. Wilkes, as well as dad's wife, Bette Deering, and Janette's mother, Rosalie Carter. I thank my sisters Elyse, Nancy and Joan, their families, and all my aunts, uncles, and cousins. This has been a difficult time for the family. I thank them for their help and I wish them well.

Thanks are due to Chuck and Gloria McDonagh, of Bahia de Kino, Sonora, who introduced us to this remarkable place, and to Maria Pinelli, also of Bahia de Kino, Sonora, for making a quiet and gracious home* available to us for months of writing over these several years.

Finally, this book has been the result of a very close and loving collaboration between myself and Carolyn Kinsman, a wonderful life partner, an excellent editor, and a remarkable person. We have worked together on this effort, in every available moment, for the past three years. Carolyn's vision and clear direction kept this project moving forward to finality. While it's true that I wrote the words, it is she who produced this beautiful tribute to my brother Steve, his wife Janette, and their son, our nephew, Eliot.

I thank her deeply for her help.

---

* The home of Bud and Gloria Brandt.

"Every little thing everyone does, changes the whole world."

Jacob Edward Rosenberger

PART I   A Tragedy in Alaska   1

PART II   Bahia de Kino   55

PART III Afterwords   151

          Epilogue   163

I Always Meant to Tell You...

PART I

A Tragedy in Alaska

A Tragedy in Alaska

Steve, you're gone now. And Janette and Eliot, too. The three of you disappeared from our lives on July 15, 2001, although your bodies were found and your ashes returned to your home in the valley of the Rio Grande. Still, you have gone from our family forever. Even months later, it somehow feels as if that small float plane that carried you north to adventure simply vanished somewhere in the vast Alaskan wilderness — a mythic ending to three precious lives .

And yet I am compelled to say something more of you. Something that tells your story to family and friends, who already know much of the story, but who may want to hear it all again. To see it written plain. People are that way. We like to hear our stories repeated. Even better, we like to see them given the imprimatur of the written word, the importance of occupying space upon a bookshelf. There is something sacred indeed about the printed word.

But how could I begin to tell of a life well lived, and too soon ended? And how to tell of three such lives? The task is enormous and it rends the heart. Yet I know that I must tell your story. You cannot be forgotten. You cannot be ignored as if you had never existed. There are nieces and nephews who will never know you well as young memories fade with age. There is a large wound in the family that remains unhealed now that you are gone. We who remain, and who knew you well, owe these moments of remembrance to you.

But where should I begin?

I had just left the house for a few minutes on an errand. It was about 5:00 p.m. on Monday the 16th of July, 2001. I'd gone a few blocks away to see a friend of ours to drop off a simple construction plan for a carport that he was already almost finished building. He had been caught by the City Building Department and "red-tagged" for building the carport without a permit. It was the second time in the last couple of years that I'd had to bail him out of a jam with the Building Department. His carpenter friend was doing a good job with the construction work, but he has never quite managed to overcome his inherent allergy to paperwork and bureaucracy. There just didn't seem to be any great necessity to get a building permit for a little two-vehicle carport that was only about 22 feet wide and about as long. When a red tag appeared on his gate, he was quick to blame the City, and those nosy neighbors who live just around the corner. The notion that it might possibly be his own fault never seemed to have occurred to him.

So he came to see me, once again, with that trademark impish grin of his — the one I'm sure his brother and parents became very well acquainted with in his youth. He asked me for help with a set of plans so he could get a permit. I'd help him again, as I had the last time. He's hard working and he's a good electrician, but before I agreed, I reminded him that I hadn't seen much of him since the last time I helped him out a couple of years ago. And I hadn't yet seen those two outside lights he'd agreed to put up for me.

There's an old Spanish *dicho*, or saying, that goes *"Dicho y Hecho."* It means "Said and Done." In this case, I was ready to modify it to *"Dicho y no Hecho."* I was reminded of another friend whose operation I had once called "The Maybe Mañana Construction Company." I'd made the decision long ago that it's better to face these harmless cross-cultural inevitabilities with a large dose of humor.

I had stopped by with the plans I had just finished, and he thanked me profusely. He asked me to stay for a beer, but I told him I couldn't because my nephew was at the house and Carolyn was putting dinner on the table. Alec was staying with us until his parents and little brother returned from a trip in Alaska, and we were celebrating his 17th birthday. Carolyn had baked a cake and I had promised I'd only be a minute. I had to go, but thanks anyway. Maybe another time. I was looking forward to dinner and conversation with my nephew.

As I pulled into our driveway, I saw a Sheriff's Department car there, but I thought little of it as there are two other residences in our compound. I thought that someone must have set off their alarm again by accident. It happens now and then, although we've all gotten much better and we hadn't done that in a while. As I stepped from my car, another vehicle — brown with official markings — came to a stop in the driveway beside me. A sign on the car read Police Chaplain. I realized he was there with bad news for someone, and now I knew it was probably me, since our parents are now quite elderly. He asked if I was Mr. Wilkes, and then he asked if we could go inside for a moment. I tried to prepare myself for the worst; in this particular case, that would not be possible.

A young female Sheriff's Deputy had given Carolyn a phone number to call in Alaska, and mentioned something about a plane crash. Carolyn made the call, to the Alaska State Police. She was badly shaken by what the man in Alaska had to tell her. Now it was up to her to tell Alec the worst news any of us had ever heard.

A few minutes later I arrived. I was stunned at the message I received, and unable to comprehend it. It was far too devastating to be possible, Steve. You were all so young and so full of promise. You and Janette had each arrived at a major turning point in your careers where the reins of influence had just been passed from a previous generation. You had each begun to make important contributions in your work. And Eliot, so young and so admired by his classmates — it simply wasn't fair for him to be gone so soon. Each of you still had many years of important and productive life ahead of you.

There were no survivors? All of you were dead? This couldn't be possible.

I looked at Alec and I reached out to hug him. His eyes were fixed in disbelief, and we hugged each other tighter than we ever had before. I held Carolyn and we all tried to make sense of this moment. The Chaplain led us in a short prayer and assured us he was available if we needed him. Then he and the Deputy quietly left us to deal with our immeasurable grief.

This couldn't be happening, could it?

Alec stepped outside to be alone for a moment and to finish adjusting his bike for a ride before dinner. The tools were still lying on the patio where he'd left them when the Chaplain arrived and we'd asked him to step inside for a moment. After the devastating news, it was time for a long and furious ride through the early evening to relieve the normal tension of seventeen-year-old muscles, the normal tension of life now mingled with a sudden explosion of unimaginable thoughts and emotions. I watched him rocket away into the dusk. There was nothing else for either of us to do or say. He needed time to be alone.

Carolyn and I wandered aimlessly through the house, each of us in an unfathomable daze as we tried to think of something to do, something to say to make this all go away, a way to fix the damage, a way to make it all right again. The mind is sometimes incapable of immediately accepting the terrible consequences of life. Sometimes it is never able to accept them. It felt to me as if we had all been sucked into a zone of madness that had destroyed all our accepted notions of life, that had turned our touchstones to dust.

Our futures had changed in an instant. I knew that my own life had now changed forever and I had no idea what it would mean to me. At that particular confusing moment, it was yet impossible for me to know.

The One to Tell Our Mother

The aftermath of a light rain was still falling, cooling the air of a July night, as I stood on our mother's porch and waited for her to return from dinner with friends. I had driven to see her shortly after I got the news and, as I stood in the cool moist air, I had time to think about the tragic message I heard only an hour or so before from a Sheriff's Deputy and a Police Chaplain.

I stood beneath her porch light and gazed through the mist, and I thought how beautiful and clean the evening was, and how the rain dripped gracefully from the boughs of that old pine tree that stands by the porch and shades most of the drive. Steve would have known what kind of pine it was, and he would also have appreciated the quiet, simple beauty of the moment. If we'd been standing there together, I would have told him about those clouds of yellow pollen that rose from a low-hanging branch I'd trimmed from that tree just a month ago. Large puffs of yellow dust rose and lingered in the air when that branch hit the ground. I realized I'd never actually thought much about pine pollen before that moment when the air was filled with it. I remembered that Steve had trimmed a few other branches from this same tree last fall. Over the years, he and I had each gotten reasonably good at trimming plants without butchering them, to make them look as if there had been no trimming at all.

I stepped off the porch into the waning drizzle and felt its cooling water on my face, and I thought about how close Steve and I had gotten during the many years that had followed our adolescent rivalries. And how we'd discovered interesting similarities in the creative ways we each dealt with life's challenges — similarities that were all the more surprising considering our very different natures. There were many good times to recall, and any bad times had long receded into the mists of memory. There would be plenty of time now to think back on all these things. And plenty of time to remember.

A Tragedy in Alaska

I shook my head once more in disbelief as I stood in the rain and I argued with the universe about the injustice of it all. These three people still had so much to offer, so much left unfinished. They couldn't be gone. Not yet. Not like this. The universe heard my stupid ravings and stared back in mocking silence.

My thoughts drifted back to what I was going to tell our Mother. It was strangely appropriate that a rain was falling this evening as I waited for the words to come, like something out of a Hollywood movie.

I wanted to tell Mom, in person, what I'd just heard. I didn't want to have to tell her over the phone that her second son, my younger brother, had been killed in the crash of a small plane north of Fairbanks, Alaska along with his wife Janette, and youngest son Elliot. Nancy Lewis, an old friend and colleague of Janette's, and an experienced bush pilot, was flying the plane. She was also killed in the crash. But how to say it? How to explain the unexplainable when she arrived, any minute now?

Mom's car pulled into the drive and she said it was a nice surprise to see me. I gave her a hug and held her close as I told her the news that still seemed so unbelievable to me. We stood there and held each other as the terrible news sank in, then we wiped our eyes and tried to dispel the shadows of this sudden reality from the recesses of our minds. I knew that my three sisters would feel the same awful pangs of disbelief. Denial and sublimation are powerful tools the mind uses in defense against terrible things such as this. Still, I couldn't imagine feeling any differently in a week, or a month, or a decade. We were all going to take a long time to recover from this event, and to get on with our own lives.

"We've been lucky, until now." Mom said between sobs. Her head was nestled into my shoulder. "Nothing like this has ever happened to us before."

Our cousin Phil died too young many years ago in a car accident on a bridge in Louisville. I still miss him to this day. I still want to hear his happy laugh, to share stories with him about the things we did when we were young. But it is not to be.

In our family, the old people die before the young, and only after a long and rewarding life. That's the way it should be, that's the way it should happen. This was not an acceptable way, or an acceptable time, for Steve, and Janette, and Elliot to die. This just wasn't right.

We talked late into the night and then it was time for me to leave. We each were left to nurse our grief as best we could. There was nothing more for us to say on this night. There is nothing that can tell you more clearly than a tragic event like this that, in the end, we are each alone in the world.

I Always Meant to Tell You...

The rain increased as I drove away in the darkness. Heavy raindrops clattered again on the overhead and washed across my windshield, fracturing the headlights of oncoming cars into brilliant shards of light. Wipers slashed across the night, and the wheels carved through puddles to send the spray crashing and drumming against the body panels. But the sound was lost in the deep and steady rain that was falling in my heart. I wiped my eyes yet again and drove homeward into the night.

A Tragedy in Alaska

Dear Eliot

July 29, 2001

Dearest Eliot,

It's been two very long weeks now since you and your parents left us forever in the plane that crashed in Alaska, and I know that I will always miss you. I just took a short nap on our living room couch with the radio playing in the background, and when I awoke I thought it had all only been a terrible dream. Then I saw a few of the many sympathy cards still lying on the counter and I felt that dull ache return to my chest. I knew then it was not just a terrible dream. I knew once again that you were gone from my life forever.

I remember all the little things about you, Eliot, that will forever have a place in my heart. Today I noticed again that annoying sound the automatic seatbelt makes in my car, and I remembered your questions. Why does it make all that noise? Well, it's wearing out. Why don't you fix it? Because it's too expensive. In fact, it's a very bad design that replaced the simple, reliable and inexpensive hand-operated belts of the past. Why did they come up with a bad design if the other one was better? Because people like to buy new cars with new gadgets. It's just a marketing thing and a lot of people fall for it. I'll never buy another car with a seat belt like this. In fact, I'm planning to replace this one with a simple hand-operated belt as soon as I can figure out a way to do it.

A month or so later you were still asking me about that noisy belt and when I was going to replace it. Something that most kids would probably have forgotten, you managed to remember; you had insistent questions that demanded clear answers. I explained that it was more complicated than I had realized. There

---

A Tragedy in Alaska

were engineering difficulties to deal with. Your penetrating eyes said that wasn't enough of an answer. What "engineering difficulties?" was the question written in your eyes. I pressed onward and tried to explain a complex engineering problem that I barely understood myself. I would have to install a bolt strong enough to absorb impact loads into the frame beside the driver's seat. I couldn't just drill a hole and put a screw in the metal because it wouldn't be strong enough. The attachment had to be as strong as the bolt itself or it would just rip out in an accident. And I couldn't tell what was behind that vinyl covering on the frame post to see how to attach it.

You listened to the intertwining threads of engineering and economics that governed my decision. I kept talking. It wasn't going to be as easy as I thought; and if I started messing with the seat belt system, the whole thing might just end up a big mess that would cost a lot of money to fix. Actually, I'd probably just leave things the way they were because it might be dangerous to try to change it. You were satisfied with that, or maybe you were just bored. And the conversation moved on to baseball, a favorite topic for us both.

The memories have been flooding in ever since your death. They're all that I have left of you now, and I cherish each one of them. I feel the intense pain of unfulfilled promise for a bright future that you will never see. One that I will never see, either.

I remember a time when you were maybe four or five years old and we were looking at a book together in the living room of your home. You stopped briefly and looked around the room, at its high viga ceiling, the plastered walls, the corner fireplace. You looked through those tall windows at the distant peak that is carefully framed. I watched your eyes as you took it all in and I didn't know what it meant. I wondered when we were going to get back to reading the book. I wondered if you'd gotten bored with the story since you'd heard it before, and if so, what I was going to do next to amuse you. It's tough to stay ahead of a five-year-old.

Then you turned to me and said, "I just want to thank you for designing us such a nice house."

I was at the very least quite surprised. I had always assumed that you were as self-centered as I remember being at your age. I've been very interested in the problems of spatial design for a very long time, but I'm not sure I ever said anything that insightful to an adult, or even thought such nice thoughts, at such an early age. I'm not sure I was even curious about where the house came from that we lived in when I was that age. I fumbled for an answer.

I Always Meant to Tell You...

"Well thank you, Eliot." I managed. "Your Mom and Dad and I worked together to design a home that would feel right on this site. We worked on it for about a year before the house was built. It takes a long time to come up with a really good design. It's not something you can rush through."

You turned back to the book. That was enough explanation for now. It would require more time for you to process it all completely. We'd get back to it another day, whenever you wanted to. But for now, we read onward through the book.

And you did come back to it, a few years later. You had other questions and observations about your environment. One day you mentioned that the eastern patio was always a nice place for family gatherings, with its surrounding garden and the way it embraced a magnificent view of the Sandia Mountains standing to the east, reaching a mile into the sky. Those weren't the words you used, but that's the essence of how I remember it. Then I asked when you enjoyed your east patio the most.

I'll admit to you now that it was a "planted" question. I wanted you to consider the reasons we designed it that way, and I wanted you to make some of your own discoveries. I wanted to share so much more with you in years to come. I wanted to answer your questions when you were ready to ask them, and to understand the answers. I had hoped to impart a little of the knowledge I've been able to accumulate over the years. I thought maybe I could save you some of the wasted effort it had cost me to gather what knowledge I had been able to accumulate. It seemed important to me and I didn't want it to be lost. Maybe that's just the egotistical affectation of an older generation, to coerce a younger generation into continuing their work. Perhaps it's a self-serving attempt at immortality. Still, I thought there was something in it for you.

You answered that you liked your eastern patio most in the afternoons when people were out there playing, talking, relaxing in the shade, watching the mountains don their evening cloak of apricot, and watermelon. You always loved people, and you enjoyed their company. You'll recall that I asked why everyone liked to sit out there in the afternoons. You grinned at the direction this interrogation was going and you said, "Because it's shady." Then I asked why it was shady, and you looked around for a moment while you considered briefly your orientation here in this small corner of the solar system. "Well, the house shades it." you said, as if to say anybody can see that, can't they. You looked again and noticed that the two-story part of the house provided very effective shading on hot afternoons here in the southwestern desert. And then you looked back at me with that broad grin of yours, a grin of recognition that maybe your uncle and your parents had

A Tragedy in Alaska

actually done something really clever, something that would bring you and others a lot of joy over the years.

I knew then that we'd have many conversations just like this one as you grew older and found your way in the world. I was very much looking forward to every one of them.

                         Love you always,
                         Your Uncle Perry

Memories

August 27, 2001

Dear Steve,

    Carolyn and I will be returning to Bahia de Kino in about a month. I don't know what I'll find there, but I feel that it's important to go there now. My memories of the time we all spent there together are so strong, the feelings are so rich, the plans I had once imagined will now be forever unfulfilled.

    I remember walking with you down that long beach eastward to Kino Viejo, the old and very funky fishing village that lives on the edge of a desert sea. It's a simple village that long predates the gringo invasion of expensive white beach homes, some of them closed against the Mexican world, and yet open to the warm and restless sea, just beyond a tall wall. Still, there are others who moved here to embrace the rich cultures of Mexico, and who are willing to learn from it. Ever since our first visit many years ago, Carolyn and I have entertained the thought that we might someday be able to live here. Or that we could afford a beach home jointly with other members of the family. In any event, it would be available to family and friends — a place to escape from the busy world that dominates our lives. I had in mind a place that would carry the echo of happy voices. Of nieces and nephews, of sisters and cousins, and of my only brother.

    I had imagined also that it would be a place where we could all explore more deeply into Mexican culture. A place where each of us might become a bit more conversant with the Spanish language, and with a people to whom we are so close, and yet so distant. Language may well be the most important key to a people and their culture, and such a broadened awareness of the world would make our lives all the richer.

A Tragedy in Alaska

There's an old Spanish *dicho* that goes, *"Una persona que habla dos lenguas, vale por dos personas."* A person who speaks two languages is worth two people. I have long felt that a basic facility with a second language, coupled with the ability to write well in one's native tongue, can be tremendously enriching to any person's life.

These thoughts were with me that evening when we all walked down the beach to dinner in Old Kino.

Our family had decided on the Marlyn Restaurant, and we set out walking a mile or two along the hard sand margins of the sea as an afternoon sun painted yet another grand sunset across a clear western sky. We'd spent an incomparable week swimming in warm seas and windsurfing on that squirley board of mine that you could never quite master. (Windsurfing favors those with a lower center of gravity and your height was a definite disadvantage.) Our brother-in-law Jimmie had taken groups of us out in his boat to fish near Tiburon Island, and your group had been blessed with spotting a small whale surface nearby to see what you were up to. And we took many long walks on that shore looking for fabulous shells and small sea creatures that had been cast upon the land.

Our trip to the Marlyn is as clear to me now as if I were staring at a photograph. We were hungry after another busy day in the sea, and we were ready for dinner. And it would be a chance for the two of us to talk. In the picture I see, you and I are striding together down that beautiful beach, our long legs leaving the rest behind; and I remember feeling like I had never been in better physical shape since those days I'd spent in boot camp way back when I was a teenager. I really don't remember what we talked about on that evening walk, or on our way back in the dark after dinner, and it doesn't even matter now. What does matter is that we were closer then than we had been in many years. I'll carry that memory with me always. And it will be especially vivid whenever I walk once again down that beach.

I find that I want to walk on that beach at Kino Bay often now as a way to be alone with you again. Yes, there's a sadness to it whenever I'm there; still, there's a great feeling of joy to it as well because, it's difficult to remember you without feeling a sense of joy. That's the way you always managed to live your life. I know there were things that troubled you about the world, Steve, and I don't want to paint you as a Pangloss or Pollyanna with no sense of the many brutal realities this life may offer. It's just that you didn't burden others with your misgivings, and your many friends especially appreciated your positive and generous nature.

I Always Meant to Tell You...

There's a poem called "We are Seven" by William Wordsworth. You'll remember, Steve, that I've always had a special fondness for Wordsworth, Keats, Shelley. Yes, it's a very strange compulsion for a leftist like me to prefer the pastoral visions of the Lake Poets over the righteous anger of, say, Ferlighetti, Corso, Ginsberg… The leftist poets have their special place in my life, and there are times when I need their truth, their anger. But mostly, at this painful moment in my life, I wish I could ignore all that. I feel the compelling need to be irrelevant to the larger picture of human endeavor, at least for a while.

These days I find myself wishing that I could waste my life near a peaceful brook…or on the shore of a gentle sea. There are times, indeed, when "the world is too much with us." And Wordsworth sums up my feelings now better than all the others, with his painfully tender work about a young girl who's lost many family members over the years, back when that was a common occurrence in the world, and yet she feels that they are all still with her. I know it's not something I'm supposed to admit, but I've never been able to read that poem without shedding a tear because of the sweet tenderness it evokes.

And that's the way I'll feel about you for the rest of my life. There have been many times already when I've begun to pick up the phone and call you. But then I remember. It's over now. I can never call you again. And we can never go for a long walk together again. I know that's the painful reality of life; but I want it all to be different, and I think Wordsworth caught the thread of it in "We are Seven:"

We Are Seven
by William Wordsworth

– A simple child,
That lightly draws its breath,
And feels its life in every limb,
What should it know of death?

I met a little cottage Girl:
She was eight years old, she said;
Her hair was thick with many a curl
That clustered round her head.

She had a rustic, woodland air,
And she was wildly clad:
Her eyes were fair, and very fair;
– Her beauty made me glad.

"Sisters and brothers, little Maid.
How many may you be?"
"How many? Seven in all," she said
And wondering looked at me.

"And where are they? I pray you tell."
She answered, "Seven are we;
And two of us at Conway dwell,
And two are gone to sea.

"Two of us in the church-yard lie,
My sister and my brother;
And, in the church-yard cottage, I
Dwell near them with my mother."

"You say that two at Conway dwell,
And two are gone to sea,
Yet ye are seven! – I pray you tell,
Sweet Maid, how this may be."

Then did the little Maid reply,
"Seven boys and girls are we;
two of us in the church-yard lie,
Beneath the church-yard tree."

"You run about, my little Maid,
Your limbs they are alive;
If two are in the church-yard laid,
Then ye are only five."

"Their graves are green, they may be seen,"
The little Maid replied,
"Twelve steps or more from my mother's door,
And they are side by side.

I Always Meant to Tell You…

"My stockings there I often knit,
My kerchief there I hem;
And there upon the ground I sit,
And sing a song to them.

"And often after sunset, Sir,
When it is light and fair,
I take my little porringer,
And eat my supper there.

"The first that died was sister Jane;
In bed she moaning lay,
Till God released her of her pain;
And then she went away.

"So in the church-yard she was laid;
And, when the grass was dry,
Together round her grave we played,
My brother John and I.

"And when the ground was white with
            snow,
And I could run and slide,
My brother John was forced to go,
And he lies by her side."

"How many are you, then," said I,
"If they are two in heaven?"
Quick was the little Maid's reply,
"O Master! we are seven."

"But they are dead; those two are dead!
Their spirits are in heaven!"
'Twas throwing words away; for still
The little Maid would have her will,
And said, "Nay, we are seven!"

A Tragedy in Alaska

And my good little buddy Eliot, I want you to know that you will also be with me forever.

I remember adventuring in the surf with you for the first time in your small life. It was something you hadn't yet sorted out how to deal with, and your normally sunny disposition was soon clouded with frustration as you sat in the warm shallow water and those insistent afternoon waves knocked you over time and again. A broad frown soon covered your face and you cried out against the persistent inconsideration of the waters. Each time you were fully concentrated on the swirling patterns of sand rushing back to the sea, another wave slapped against you, knocking you over and filling your mouth with sandy, brackish water. Your eyes appealed to me, as a higher power, to stop those waves so you could concentrate on the fascinating and fluid patterns of the sand. But I was just as helpless in the face of Nature. And then I realized we needed to turn this natural encounter with the wind and the water into a game of some kind. I sat with you in the surf and waited for the next wave to crash over us.

"We just got blasted!" I yelled above the roaring surf, and fell over into a ridiculously exaggerated pile of flailing limbs. You loved seeing your uncle look ridiculous, and you came out of the surf sputtering, and laughing at my antics. Then the receding water tugged me over the other way just in time to get "Blasted!" again by the next wave. And you laughed again at the absurdity of it all.

Later in the week, I walked past where you were playing in the edge of the surging water with a new young friend. The waves washed over both of you, and neither of you seemed to notice. You each just rocked with the waves, your game uninterrupted by the forces of nature.

I had planned to return many times with you, Eliot, and with your family, to that gentle beach at Kino Bay. I planned to tell you, as uncles do, of these memories of mine in years to come, after you and I had each grown much older. And maybe after you'd had children of your own to enjoy special moments with. I just wanted us to walk together again someday on the beach at Kino Bay, and remember those moments. And laugh together again.

Dear Eliot

August 28, 2001

Dearest Eliot,

These days, I often find myself recalling times that you and I spent together. I can't help it, I just think about you a lot these days. In fact, I think about you and your mother and father almost constantly.

Today something reminded me of that time on a chilly late afternoon when I took you to a place where you and I could get a distant look — if we looked real hard — at both Los Angeles and Chicago. I think you were about seven years old.

It was sometime in the Fall, as I recall it now, and we were on our way someplace; but I don't remember where. It wasn't part of the adventure, so I guess it wasn't important to me. I had taken an unusual and circuitous route, and you wondered just what we were doing as I pulled to the side of a quiet street in the descending dusk. The whole thing seemed suspicious to you, like I was trying to trick you into eating strange food or something.

Hop out, I said, and don't bother to lock the door. We'll be right back. You had a puzzled look on your face at this latest antic of an eccentric uncle.

I zipped my jacket against the slight breeze. Slight and cold and persistent. You wore a t-shirt and a ball cap, and you said you were fine. You never wore much else — even in the middle of winter. Your father and I, two tall and slender guys, always found that remarkable.

We walked along the deserted road, hand in hand up a slight grade, until we stopped at the very top. And there before us was what we had come to see, lying right at our feet. Two cold, gleaming rails reflected the fading sunlight and the lights of the awakening city along their strong and slightly curved spines as they

---

A Tragedy in Alaska

stretched onward into infinity. Light collected like jewels along each edge and reflected outward into the night. I stared at those two steel rails, and I marveled at the magic they contained. I thought again of the many trains they had carried over the past hundred years, the people and the freight they had delivered, the mysterious and unknown places they connected throughout the nation.

You looked at me quizzically and wondered what we were doing here, standing in the dark like this, looking at a pair of empty rails, fastened with stout spikes into heavy oaken ties, nestled in a deep bed of crushed stone.

I pointed down those rails to the horizon, and I looked toward Los Angeles. You looked down my outstretched arm.

"Do you see it?" I asked. You looked up at me to see if I was actually serious.

"There in the distance." I said, "At the end of these rails. Connected to the very end of the rails we're standing on. Can you see the tall buildings? And that's the ocean just beyond. That's LA. Right there at the end of these rails."

You looked dubiously in my direction and asked, "Can we go now?"

"No, no," I said. "Wait just a minute, and imagine. If you caught a ride on a flat car headed in that direction, you'd end up in Los Angeles in a day or so. You see, you're no longer bound by your horizons. You can go anywhere you want. There's a large, magical world out there just at the end of these two rails, and it's all yours, if you want it. You can go there some day."

You had a look on your face that said you'd probably rather just fly there with your family and go see Disneyland. You couldn't imagine the strange and compelling romance of riding the rails, not at your tender age.

I took your hand and we turned to face the opposite direction. A car rolled over the crossing with its headlights on. The driver glanced at us, and wondered what we were doing standing out there in the dark. I could see it briefly in his face. His taillights disappeared down the road.

"That's Chicago." I pointed into the fading distance. "It's right there, just beyond the horizon. You can almost touch it. You can see the old Monadnock Building, the very first skyscraper ever built. There's the Sears Tower, and the Carson Pirie Scott Building. And there's the lake just beyond, Lake Michigan. It's so wide you can't see across it, and it's just a lake — it's not even an ocean. There's more interesting stuff there than you can imagine. Someday I hope you'll follow those rails to the end. And you'll see what I mean."

You were ready to leave, and so was I. But I knew that in a few years I'd bring you back to the crossing and we'd look down those tracks again together. I knew you'd see Chicago then. And Los Angeles.

I Always Meant to Tell You...

I knew you thought that evening was more than a little strange. At your age, I don't know if I'd have appreciated such a metaphorical fieldtrip, either. But I thought that someday I'd get you to join us for a train trip to Chicago on a sleeper car, like people used to do in the old days before everything got too easy and we lost most of our regional culture. Aunt Carolyn would travel with us, and a buddy of yours could go along, or maybe a girlfriend. Maybe you'd be on your way back to college somewhere in the East. Or maybe you'd be married by then, and your wonderful wife would be traveling with us.

Maybe we'd go in the early fall, and we'd slowly leave the mountains of New Mexico behind as that long train carved its way to the east. We'd cross those vast grasslands of the high plains, the fabled sea of grass. And we'd slice through thousands of acres of cornfields standing tall and gold and ripe in the sun, the golden wealth of the American heartland. And I'd probably bore you by pointing out the historical and geographic accident that is America. There are only a few places in the entire world where the accidental convergence of climate, altitude, and flat land creates vast agricultural wealth like the heartland of America. We are the beneficiaries of it, whether we deserve it or not.

There is much a person can see from an airplane, but it is impossible to fully experience the vastness and variety of this land from the air. The flavor of her small towns and the intricacies of her commerce can only be experienced from the ground. And train travel gives a unique perspective that few Americans take the time to enjoy any more.

I wanted you to feel the magic in those rails on that chilly evening when we stopped at the railroad crossing. And I knew we'd take that trip someday, my young buddy. I just knew we'd do it together, someday.

A Tragedy in Alaska

An Unexpected Reconciliation

August 29, 2001

Steve,

    I could see it in your face. You were as amazed as I was by a turn of events we were privileged to witness at the June wedding of Carolyn's son Jay and his beautiful bride Ann. We were standing to one side, watching our Mom and Dad actually talking over old times and laughing together for the first time since their divorce in 1972. I think it happened around 1972, and I'm sure you wouldn't remember the date any better than I do. I believe time has always been a continuum for both of us, and there were no neat divisions in our limited understanding of the universe to peg these important events on. Why is it so important to remember the exact date, anyway?

    Except that it was the year I got divorced too.

    And it was the year you got divorced.

    And it was the year our sister Elyse also got divorced.

    We could ask her what year it was. She'd remember.

    We were quite a bunch that year, the four of us, weren't we? I remember once we were together at Mom's house for Sunday dinner and some Canasta. We just looked at each other, shaking our heads and laughing wryly at a remarkable string of events that had left each of us suddenly single in the same year.

    Meanwhile, our father was living alone, trying to make sense of that personal hell into which he'd just entered as a consequence of divorce. But we kids were too young and absorbed by our own failures to understand his pain.

    Were we failures? Or were we each moving forward with our lives after shedding some unbearable weight? And what of those who hadn't actually

---

A Tragedy in Alaska

chosen divorce, but had it forced upon them? Was this, somehow, a good thing for them, too?

And what did our two youngest, still unmarried, sisters think of all this? It can't have seemed like anything short of an ominous portent to them both, perhaps a new, unhappy, family tradition they might be destined to continue.

I didn't know at the time what any of this meant to me, to you, or to the others, yet I know now that it was an unfortunate opportunity for a new attempt at a better life, for a more productive relationship with a new person. What was past was now over, although not entirely unlamented. But I think we all knew deep inside that, after all this pain, the world would present us with a better choices. It would be a slow process, and we had to recognize the opportunities as they appeared. We had to be ready to develop the relationships that materialized.

And that was indeed what happened. For each of us.

That was when you met your life-mate, Janette, a very bright young woman who was your intellectual equal and who would be the mother of your children.

As Jay and Ann's wedding approached, you and I planned that neither of our parents would be sitting without one of us in the next chair. I was nervous when I called Dad to ask if this would be a good thing — to see his ex-wife at the wedding. I was surprised when he said, without hesitation, that it wasn't a problem. Still, I was apprehensive. We both knew it wouldn't bother Mom, but we still didn't really know how Dad would take it.

You picked up Mom at her house, and I met Dad and Bette in front of Ann's parent's house, where the wedding would occur. The Plan was to seat them separately, with plenty of space between. If things went well, they could exchange cordialities at the food line, or something like that. What happened next was a complete surprise to both of us.

You found a place for you and Mom to sit in the middle of a row toward the back. I collected Dad and Bette in the front yard and escorted them to the back yard. As I attempted to steer them to the other side of the seating area, Bette saw Mom, took Dad's arm, and walked over to sit down right next to her. They began a wonderful conversation that included Dad, who had to lean across Bette due to his poor hearing. Bette, always very practical, had apparently thought this estrangement had gone on long enough and wanted to get it behind everyone. You and I were amazed to watch our parents getting along famously after so many years of separation. They had been childhood sweethearts, and they knew each other's family well. Many in each family were gone now, and the time had come for a reconciliation. There was much to talk about, years to remember.

And suddenly there we were, you and I, standing on the sidelines watching an event unfold that we never really thought would occur. Or even could occur, based on hard feelings long buried in the bitter past. I'm glad you and I saw it happen, together, before the day our aging parents passed away. As we all must.

I'm especially glad you saw it happen, before your own early death.

But I need to tell you what has happened since then. I know you'll never read this now, but I need to tell you anyway. Life would be so much easier if I could just believe that you were up there somewhere, reclined on a cloud and watching the foolishness of we mortals who are left here below to deal with all the various predicaments we've gotten ourselves into. I can imagine that you would see the choices and their consequences far sooner than we could, but you couldn't predict human behavior — and that would be the amusing part of it all. You would peek over the edge of your cloud and see which path we've finally decided to take, and you'd just cover your eyes while we bumbled into the next disaster like some endless Laurel and Hardy movie. I know you'd appreciate the humor in it. You'd look down at the results, and most of the time you'd just shake your head and smile that wry smile of yours as we tried to find a way out of the next mess we'd created. I'm going to miss that smile now for the rest of my own life.

It would be easier if I could believe all that, and sometimes, for a while, I think I actually do believe it. And I'll admit that sometimes it feels good when I can do that. Maybe it's only a mental trick, to enter a hidden place behind those tall walls that guard the kingdom of memory. But mostly I just think about the very real fact that I won't ever see you and Janette and Eliot again.

And the now familiar dull ache of resignation returns once again.

A Tragedy in Alaska

To Janette

August 28, 2001

Dearest Janette,

    I remember your beautiful voice:
    "Hi, guys. This is Janette."

I can still hear it, bright and clear, on the answering machine, embraced with that big warm smile you always kept tucked just inside. I was sorry we weren't home to get your message, but you were going to be back in another week anyway. We could catch up with all of your considerable adventures then and look at the pile of pictures we knew you'd have.

    "We're calling from Whitehorse, in the Yukon." you said. "Just wanted to let you know we're having a great time seeing the North Country, although Eliot's probably getting a little tired of all the driving. We should be in Fairbanks tomorrow, and my friend Nancy is going to take us on a plane ride up to a lake she knows about just above the Arctic Circle near the Gates of the Arctic National Park. That should be fun."

    Fun indeed. It sounded like a great adventure, the Trip of a Lifetime. I was looking forward to the day, just a few years hence, when we could also hop in our old van and have a chance to see the nation's biggest state. We were looking forward to comparing notes with you then.

    "Sorry we missed you. Hope everything is going well with Alec. Tell him we miss him. We'll call again from Hugh and Nancy's house when we get back from the plane trip."

    You left Hugh and Nancy's phone number in case we needed to get in touch with them for any reason.

A Tragedy in Alaska

Then you said goodbye. We were going to pick you up at the airport when you returned, and we could hardly wait to hear your tales about those great lands to the north. It was wonderful to hear your happy voice again on our answering machine.

I couldn't imagine at the time that I would never hear your voice again.

You joined our large family, Janette, when you and Steve began your courtship, dancing to the music that rang from the stage of the old Golden Inn in those golden years of the 1970s. Steve played there often with the Jug Band, and that may have been the place you met. I don't remember the story, and now it's too late to ask.

You, an only child, were guarded at first when faced with the five of us. We were our usual boisterous, querulous selves, unaware of the quiet environment of your childhood. At times, you appeared almost overwhelmed by the sheer numbers of in-laws you suddenly had to deal with. Yet together, we learned to love and respect each other, and I know you eventually felt accepted as a full member of our family.

During your brief time with us you were passionately in love, and it wore very well on you. Passionately in love with Steve, with your two sons, and with the world. In February of 2001 you took a little time for yourself, a well deserved break with some of your women friends at a place in Belize. I know you must have thought a great deal about this trip before you went. You were always modest in your life, and I know you realized you were one of the world's privileged people just to consider such a trip. And you wondered if it was a good thing to leave your family for a week to be far away in a tropical jungle.

A week with close friends in the jungle was a very good idea, and it allowed you the quiet space to express your thoughts more poetically than ever before. Your intimate connection to the world was expressed so beautifully in one of several pieces you shared with us:

A Collect

Sacred being that blesses the morning
That created all the four legged and the two legged beings,
Remind me to live each day fully awake to the sacred within myself
and all creatures
That I might be blessed with glimpses of eternity as I move through
the day.

I will always remember you well, Janette, your generosity and warmth, your grace and intelligence. And your concern for others less fortunate, a concern that was quietly expressed but deeply held, and acted upon without fanfare. You were part of our family for almost half your life. I can remember when Steve brought you to meet the family at one of those Sunday night dinners that Mom held while we were in college and for years afterward. Those Sunday dinners were how Mom kept us well fed and connected to each other at a time in our lives when it would be very easy to get swept up in the minutiae of existence. Your eyes were filled with pride and love each time you looked upward at my tall brother, and we were all pleased to see this. You expressed it well in another work you composed there in the Belizean jungle:

For Steve

We fit together
Both passionate
One looking around
      One looking at the horizon
One planting flowers
      One off on an adventure
One laughing
      One searching for the right
      Path with determination
A lived life
      An examined life
Tall, short
Faith in people, faith in God
We fit together, my lover.

And your sons, those two young guys who filled your busy life with challenge and delight. Although you were a working mother with tremendous responsibility, they were constantly on your mind. Especially whenever the requirements of your job demanded that you'd be far away. That was when you missed them most. You had strong feelings and a unique relationship with for both of these young guys. And your feelings were especially strong for Alec, the oldest, and always the most challenging:

A Tragedy in Alaska

For Alec

Mother bear
Growling fiercely at the world
Leave my son alone! Please.

Mother otter
Cracking shells on my tummy.
Come little son, have one.

Mother eagle
Courage, wisdom, strength in flight.
My son, it is yours.

My son,
Discoverer of earth's treasures
Not seen by the rest of us.
Seeing the world in colors and images
I don't see.
Feeling the psychic world in sharp clarity,
Archetypes swimming in your mind.
Sometimes persecuted without.
Sometimes persecuted within.
Strong emotions always.
A good heart, a God heart.

And, though you didn't say so in your writings, I feel that this piece may have been written to Eliot, who we once took to see "Crouching Tiger...":

My Son
(After seeing "Crouching Tiger..." movie)

How do I love thee?
I would climb a mountain
and hurl myself off the precipice
wishing you freedom from all that haunts you.

I Always Meant to Tell You...

I would become a mother bear
ready to defend my cub
against a pack of angry wolves
> *wolves of societal norms*
> *expectations*
> *sequential tasks*
> *mathematical numbers*
> *square boxes*
> *square holes*
> *people pretending the patina*
> > *of their life is who they are*
> *perfect pretenders*
> *perfect persecutors*

The love I hold for you makes me bigger than life
raging blindly
one thought
save my son.

You had a very quiet and contemplative side that occasionally called you to retreat from life and to spend close time with those you loved:

Brief Poem

Big parties
> *Don't work.*
One-on-one
> *That's where the answers lurk.*
I don't have to be at the party to Love You.

Someone, I don't know who, wrote this message as part of a fax that arrived on Steve's machine after your death:

In Belize we discussed that the root word for "Blessing" is seeing. We used the practice of "seeing/blessing" each other with our eyes. We decided to become guerillas (sp.) for blessing — giving people love whether they knew it or not. Janette wrote this:

> *Blessing with your eyes*
> *Recognized*
> *Unrecognized*
> *Matters not.*

Janette, I was never before aware of your considerable ability with the written word. As with the rest of your life, you refrained from self-promotion in your writing. But you had an impressive ability to express yourself powerfully and well in poetic form, and I'm very sorry your voice has been stilled. You were truly one of the more remarkable people I have ever been privileged to have known.

I can never forget you.

Dear Eliot

Accepting Applications for Cook, Assistant Cook/Deckhand, Engineer and Deckhands aboard the 103-foot gaff-rigged square topsail ketch, Hawaiian Chieftain. Teaching ability in outdoor education, hospitality industry experience, good people skills an advantage. Hard working with a great attitude a must. Minimum 4 months full-time contracts. Salary and room/board commensurate with position and experience. April-October conducting educational programs, summer day camps and public/private charters in San Francisco Bay. November-March touring southern California ports with the 110-foot Brig Lady Washington. Please forward your resume to: Alina McIntyre, Hawaiian Chieftain, 3020 Bridgeway, Suite 266, Sausalito CA 94965. Phone: (415) 706-3214. Fax: (415) 331-9415. Email: alina@tallship.vip.best.com.

August 29, 2001

Dearest Eliot,

    I thought of you when I saw this ad in the September 2001 issue of *Latitude 38*, a Bay Area sailing rag I've subscribed to for many years now. I especially thought of you when I got to the part about "...good people skills an advantage." And that line about "Hard working with a great attitude a must." I thought they had described you perfectly. That's how you led your life already, and I know you would have been even better at it in another ten years when were old enough to email Alina McIntyre about those jobs aboard the Hawaiian Chieftain.
    I have to confess that in the short time I knew you, I was developing a serious interest in the many successes that I knew would be yours in years to come. I would never have been accused of having "good people skills" at your young age. I was hoping, just maybe, you would sign aboard a tall sailing ship

A Tragedy in Alaska

for a season and I'd have the great pleasure of living vicariously through your adventures as you helped hoist an acre of sail in the air to fly before the wind, and as you visited ports of call along the California coast. Through your voyages, I'd follow your progress and revisit the fabled "Age of Sail" on one of the greatest of the "tall ships."

But it was not to be. I'm very sorry now that such rich voyages to adventure can never come to pass, for you and for myself, my young nephew and my very close friend.

                              Love always,
                              Your Uncle Perry

The World Trade Center Disaster

September 14, 2001

    We'll be going to Mexico in about a week, Steve — as we had planned long before the crash that took the lives of you and Janette and Eliot.

    Suddenly this year, I'm very much looking forward to staying in a small and simple home on a long curving beach with no phone, no television, and no other distractions — except for a small radio. There's a very good station at the *Universidad de Sonora* in Hermosillo that broadcasts excellent classical music, jazz, and conversation. I can easily let it fade into the background, since my Spanish abilities are such that I have to concentrate in order to understand all the words and phrases. Maybe some day I'll spend enough time in Latin America to actually speak the language decently. I think I've been working all my life toward the elusive goal of complete freedom, the kind of freedom necessary to indulge my curiosities. Sometimes I think I've spent most of my life as an unwilling contributor to the greater good of society, at least to the extent that it requires adherence to the dictates of others.

    But that's not the main reason I'm looking forward to this month of solitude. I want an extended and uninterrupted period to think about your life, to write about the times we spent together, to write a very long letter to you. And to think of sweet lovely Janette. And of my buddy Eliot. I know that you would not be at all amazed at the number of people who thought of Eliot as their very close buddy. You knew him well, and better than any of the rest of us; and he was more than just your son. He was your close buddy, too.

    My main goal now is to spend some significant time trying to release those feelings deep inside that have found no real time for expression in the two months since you died. I need the time and the space to think, and to write. The world is too much with us, as the sage once said. Especially just lately.

This week, just as we prepare to leave, has been a shockingly strange week, so far, not only for me but for many others. This is the week in which two jet airliners smashed into the the twin towers of the World Trade Center in Manhattan, sending both towers crashing to the ground and killing thousands of people. It was a direct blow against the corrupt policies of Corporate America and their defenders in the Pentagon, but the damage was much more horrific than anyone could have imagined and the world was stunned at the outcome. Like most other human disasters, this one is also likely to be turned to political advantage. The lessons are likely to be ignored yet again.

I've thought a lot lately about those panic-stricken passengers roaring unknowingly toward their deaths. And I thought of you. The hijacked passengers who crashed into those buildings had the very real advantage of not being able to stare forward into the certainty of their imminent doom. You Janette and Eliot, and Nancy, your friend and pilot, were denied even that small measure of comfort as your plane suddenly stalled and hurtled earthward on that final fatal day in July of 2001.

I can't begin to imagine it.

The First Lines of a Novel

September 15, 2001

Dear Steve,

    We were together on a Sunday morning, just a couple of weeks before your big cross-country road trip. You were all very excited about it. We had gathered to discuss when Alec would be returning from BMX Camp in Pennsylvania to stay with us. You, Janette, and Eliot would drive him there, and continue your long land voyage back westward across the northern tier of the entire country. In Montana, you'd head even farther north to see Alaska. You would travel in the old "Chevy Subdivision" — Dave Barry's name for that huge, gas-guzzling, vehicle you bought for the trip. It was unlike you to own such a thing, but the realities of teenager-dom had mandated it. There was a small TV set facing the second seat, and way in the back there was a complete, separate, radio system with headphones and no speakers. A kid could spend hours back there plugged into "Teenage Nirvana" without bothering everybody else in the car. The guy who designed this rolling pleasure palace clearly understood his market.

    You explained Alec's itinerary and answered our questions. Alec would be arriving home a week ahead of the rest of the family and he'd stay at our place. It would be a test for Carolyn and me, but we'd have fun. We just hadn't had a teenager around for quite a while.

    We were in the living room of our small solar home when I brought up the subject of first lines from novels because I wanted to read Eliot the first paragraph of *Treasure Island*. I had recently bought a copy of that old edition with the famous N. C. Wyeth illustrations so I could read it to him after the trip. At

A Tragedy in Alaska

nine years of age, I felt he was ready for this classic adventure yarn. He had a new fascination with pirates, and he was spending a lot of time chanting, "Fifteen men on a dead man's chest! Yo ho ho and a bottle of rum! Drink and the Devil had done for the rest! Yo ho ho and a bottle of rum!"

I was impressed that he even knew the second verse.

In the future, I'd teach Eliot to sail a small boat we bought, and I hoped he'd share my fascination with sailing craft. It's a strange passion for someone who's grown up in the desert, and I needed the company of a fellow addict. I planned to spend significant time on the water with Eliot.

And now he's gone, and I'm left with only a gnawing sense of loss.

Desert Flowers

September 16, 2001

    It's September now, Steve.

    The late flowers of the high desert have come to life again, as they do each year after the arrival of the rains. And the temperature has fallen to a point where the evenings are refreshingly cool once again. A carpet of simple desert flowers covers the land again this Fall.

    The apple trees have delivered their bounty of fruit — small, red, crisp, and savory. The fields are ripe, and the smell of roasting chiles is in the air. It's the reaffirmation of an ancient annual ritual, one of joy, renewal, and abundance. I recall many times when you and I spoke of the simple pleasures of Fall's bounty and the beauty of the land around us. I think it was your favorite season.

    I especially miss hearing your voice this year when the holiday season arrives and the family spends significant time together. I miss your wisdom and your appreciation of the beauty.

    Today I passed a cluster of bright pink primroses mingled with little gray-leaved buttercups. I don't know their proper name, and I thought of you as I looked at their delicate beauty. I was sure you knew their name. I wish there were some way that you could tell it to me now.

    I wish I could ask you once again.

A Tragedy in Alaska

A Sign I Happened to See

September 17, 2001

Dear Steve,

    I passed a sign today that was posted at a fast food place on North Fourth Street, and I thought you would appreciate it. It read "God bless America tacos 2 for 99¢."
    It's clear they meant to honor those who perished last week in that astounding attack on the World Trade Center in Manhattan. Yet it struck me as oddly tacky, this close mingling of sentiment and commerce. Would it really hurt to cut back, just briefly, on the advertising? It also seemed terribly ironic, since those who piloted the planes also did so "in the name of God."
    Somehow, this all reminded me of you, although I don't need much reminding these days. I just thought this message, and a lot of other things going on these days, would appeal to your well-refined sense of the ridiculous.
    For example, there was some Republican running for office in Texas who used the occasion to cast aspersions on the patriotism of his opponent. One of his large campaign ads appeared with an American flag across the background behind a soldier wearing a uniform that looked oddly wrong, with patches that aren't normally seen on American uniforms. Turns out it was a picture of some German general that a layout artist had mistakenly stuck in there. If this Republican had ever been in the service, he would have recognized the problem. It seems fitting that the self-serving blunder of this particular scoundrel quickly made the national news.
    Then the Bush administration used this tragic opportunity to sneak through an appointment of one of the nastiest characters involved with this country's long mercenary wars in Central America. He's now the United States Ambassador to the United Nations.

A Tragedy in Alaska

Amid the pain of that still-unbelievable suicide attack on the World Trade Center, the usual opportunists have exploited the occasion for cynical purposes. They apparently have no shame. It's only a continuing game to these guys. And we're still just pawns in the game.

But then there are poor souls who innocently create unintentional language that an ungenerous soul might call tacky under the circumstances. I can picture your wry smile, and I know you would understand that language ability has little to do with someone's deeply-held and sincere emotions. Still, they sometimes offer us a darkly humorous break from the pain.

Throughout our lives I could always count on you to appreciate the intellectual qualities of a malapropism, or a good pun... regardless of the withering opprobrium of those unwillingly blessed with the opportunity to attend such precious moments of wit.

Now that you're gone, who can I share these moments with? Who else will ever understand?

Point of Impact

Somewhere in the Alaska wilderness, on a lake about a hundred thirty miles north of Fairbanks, the engine of a small plane roared to life and split the ancient silence. Its occupants were buckled in and ready to return to the city after a long summer day of hiking and berry picking in the far northern woods.

Their plane taxied away from the shore, its long pontoons carving an arc through still waters, readying for takeoff. Then the propeller sliced arcs into the air and the little plane skimmed across the surface, its speed increasing as the wind gathered beneath its wings until it regained the freedom of the air. It rose high above the clean cold waters, crossed a pine-covered shoreline far below, and left the lake behind. They traveled inland and soared high above a broad and untouched green landscape. Then there was a sputter of engine and momentary quiet returned to the wilderness.

Air rushed over the wingtips and past a stalled propeller while the pilot worked frantically to restart the engine, to bring the stalled plane around, perhaps to glide it back to the lake. She was an experienced pilot in the ways of the Alaskan back country and it was her only choice, although she knew she probably didn't have the airspeed and the altitude to make it. Those long pontoons that once took so lightly to the water now dragged heavily through the air and pulled her plane downward to the earth.

The people aboard watched this sudden change in their afternoon flight to a quiet lake beneath a gentle sky. They knew that something was now terribly wrong. It's impossible to know their thoughts in the last seconds of their lives, their fates sealed when they stepped from that remote and quiet lakeshore into the plane. Maybe there was a scream of utter panic as their plane lost airspeed, and fell downward. Few of us could maintain our composure under such circumstances.

There was a brief splintering sound as the plane impacted on the earth. Then a deep and natural silence returned to the northern woods.

A gentle breeze sang once again through the short and hardy pines that survive the bitter cold of an Alaska winter. Ducks called again from the rich waters they visit each summer. Bees and small butterflies caressed brilliant little flowers in a meadow. A moose lowered its head once again and grazed on water weeds growing in shallow marshes.

And the Universe continued.

It's difficult to even think about the final moments of Steve, Janette, Eliot, and their friend Nancy. But there are questions that must be laid to rest. I wish there were a better way, but I think the questions must be asked, even if there is no possibility of an answer. I need to do that for closure. It's the only way I can deal with the pain.

What could have caused this crash?

Was it pilot error?

Apparently that's one of the first questions the National Transportation Safety Board, the NTSB, always asks. Nancy Lewis was a cautious pilot with considerable flying experience in the Alaskan back-country. Although pilot error is always a possibility, it wasn't likely in this case.

Was it the weather?

There was an undeveloped roll of film at the crash site. Steve always took pictures, and these were probably his. The last 20 or so photos showed a happy expedition through blueberry patches to some nearby and interesting rock formations called granite tors. They showed Eliot enjoying a last swim in the cold water of that northern lake. They showed a small plane nuzzled against a quiet shore. All of these pictures, including those at the end of the roll taken just before boarding, show a sunny and benevolent sky filled with small puffy white clouds.

Was there a dangerous approach to the lake through steep mountain passes? Those same pictures of a happy afternoon trek show only low hills sloping gradually away from the lakeshore in all directions. There are a few mountains, far in the distant background.

Was there a mechanical problem? The plane looked very well-tended in the last of the photographs, as it sat nosed up to the lakeshore. It was a plane that the owner was very proud of. Nancy's husband, Hugh Rose, has also spoken of the new $60,000 engine that was recently installed in the plane.

Good appearance is no indicator of good maintenance, but that's not a likely answer here. Everyone who knew Nancy said she was meticulous and serious about every pre-flight checkout. And no-one can imagine Steve and Janette risking their own lives or the life of their son flying in a derelict plane. They simply didn't associate with people who took those kinds of needless risks. There is no evidence of poor maintenance here.

Was there a distraction that could have led to a fatal mistake? Did the pilot turn the wrong switch or pull the wrong lever when someone made a funny remark, or pointed out an interesting tree or animal somewhere on the ground below? That will always remain a possibility.

Aircraft engines drink fuel at a heavy rate. Did the main fuel tank suddenly run dry on that sunny afternoon? Was there an auxiliary fuel tank? Did it go unnoticed in the fun of a sunny summer day at the Arctic Circle that the main tank was almost empty, and it was time to switch to the spare before taxiing across the lake for takeoff?

Nancy Lewis was a careful pilot. She probably switched tanks before she began taxiing across the lake for a takeoff. Or maybe she had enough gas left for takeoff and planned to drain that tank before switching over. Yet, when the engine started to cough, were they too low in altitude for the fuel from the auxiliary tank to reach those hungry cylinders in time?

Was there contamination in that second tankload of fuel? Surely the NTSB checked the remaining fuel for contamination. Surely they checked the in-line fuel filters for clogging. That must be a basic step in any investigation.

Had someone tampered with the plane? The question must be asked, yet it's hard to imagine. What would be the reason? Who would do such a thing? Who would stand to gain?

As some point during those early moments of the flight, a serious problem became apparent to the pilot and her passengers. The engine had coughed into silence, and the propeller that had always reliably sliced through the air just beyond that broad windshield had stopped turning. All four of those aboard were suddenly aware of a great silence that engulfed them — a profound and disturbing silence broken by the sound of wind rushing over the wings and past the fuselage. A silence broken only by the efforts of the pilot as she tried to restart the engine, and turn her plane back toward the lake hoping there was sufficient glide-time to make it. I can't get that image out of my mind.

There was little room to land safely on the rugged ground below. There were few choices available during those brief moments that did not pose additional danger to her passengers as Nancy Lewis hoped for just enough glide-time to bring her small plane back to the soft surface of the lake. The level of apprehension in the cockpit must have been palpable as these thoughts raced through each mind.

At this point Steve might have said something like, "Well, maybe you'll get to go swimming again, Eliot, while we figure out what's wrong with the plane." Eliot would have laughed and said "Cool!" They were each very good at keeping spirits up and helping others to avoid concentrating on the worst that could happen. Imagine the stories they would tell their family and friends when they returned, if they could only survive one more adventure in what had already been a very interesting vacation.

For her part, Nancy was surely telling them all that she was looking for a decent place to land, if they couldn't make it to the lake. Either way, it would be a rough landing.

But a small plane carrying a full load of passengers, crippled by the additional aerodynamic drag of two long pontoons, would not have a large margin of error on this particular day. At some point, the airspeed fell below a critical level, and Nancy's little plane plummeted downward to the hard and unforgiving surface of the earth.

The plane was not completely destroyed, as there was no fire damage at the site, so there was at least the possibility of some answers. But there would be no answers hidden in the silence of the wreckage that lay on an Alaskan hillside. Many small plane crashes remain mysteries that are never solved. In this case, the information gathered may help others to avoid a similar fate, and that's probably the best we can ever hope for. And then, they may be no answers at all.

There's no point in assessing blame. It won't do anything to return our family to us.

At this time, about three months after the crash, the preliminary report of the accident is still posted on the NTSB web site. We wait for the final NTSB Report to tell us what happened in those last few fatal moments.

Yet there may never be anything else to add to the preliminary report.

Note: See Appendix for final NTSB report. The pictures posted with the final report showed a remarkably intact aircraft, but with clear structural damage, resting right side up on an open sloping hillside covered with short brush.

A Meeting with Alec

I am at a meeting at the Career Enrichment Center with Alec and his teachers. The Fall semester is underway. We will try to see if there is any way to reach him now that his family is gone, to convince him to finish his high school education. Alec knows he doesn't really have to worry about making a living now. He knows there's a trust fund at his disposal in a few more years, so what's the use of putting up with these teachers any longer anyway.

I don't have any idea what I'm supposed to do or say at this meeting. I guess I'm supposed to be the wise uncle here, to give Alec a good reason to stay in school, to connect with this kid in some significant way. I just hope I don't say something terribly stupid.

The fact is that not one of us, not even his teachers, has any idea what's going on in his head. We don't really know how to reach this kid who remains so closed to the adult world that surrounds, and engulfs, him. There was a time when I identified very closely with Alec, with his constant losing battles against authority. I remember those days in my own youth. But things have now changed forever. I don't know that we'll ever again have a common base of experience.

The Career Enrichment Center specializes in kids like Alec who don't fit into the regular curriculum. One of his teachers clarified the situation for me, "Often, the best we can hope for is to turn potential murderers into car thieves." Nobody here expects that of Alec. They like Alec and think he's a smart, decent kid who just needs to be refocused in a positive direction. Still, it's a tough bunch he's managed to find himself with.

At the CEC, they try to lessen the damage these kids inflict on society, their families, themselves. These teachers are society's last chance to reach these kids in their teenage years, and sometimes they fail. Often they fail. It's a tough job.

On one wall of the room there's a quote from someone named Robert Ingersol, and it seems appropriate for the moment:

"In nature there are no rewards or punishments, only consequences."

It's hard for humans to understand that the world will not much notice our passing. Generally, we're too self-centered to consider the possibility of a world without us. I often thought in my youth about those thousands, even millions, of innocent people young and old who were swept up in an unstoppable tide of events and perished in one of the world's many wars over the centuries of our existence. And I have wondered how the world might have changed if they had lived to grace us with their intelligence. I have wondered how much farther we all may have gotten if they had lived their lives to the fullest.

And now I think of you, Alec. And I think of consequences. Have we learned anything at all from several million years of so-called evolution?

Have you?

Have I?

Adobe Siding

September 19, 2001

"This is the Acme Adobe Siding Company and we're in your neighborhood today!" I can hear your voice even now as I write this, Steve — sonorous, rich, with a broad smile implied in the texture of every word. I wish that I'd saved just one of those messages that you left on the answering machine. But at the time there was no reason to. I knew there'd be another one soon.

"We have a special offer today to introduce you to the unique properties of our patented line of Adobe Siding products." you continued. "Want that Santa Fe look, but can't afford it? We'll just glue that look right onto the outside of your house at a fraction of the cost of remodeling. Call today for a free in-home demonstration. We'll even sweep our mess off the floor before we leave."

After the gag lines, you'd ask if Carolyn and I would be available to catch one of Eliot's Little League baseball games. Or maybe Alec was bustin' some new moves on his BMX bike, or some new licks on his electric guitar. He had gotten to the point where he could rip off a pretty good version of "Smoke on the Water." At least he had that signature riff down, anyway. And he was really into John Fogarty since he'd discovered a couple of old LPs you had in the closet. You and I still weren't up to his musical standards, but at least we weren't yet hopelessly relegated to the depths of old-fogydom. It was a tough sentence for two guys who still thought we were decent rock-and-rollers.

You were very proud of both those guys, your sons, and it always showed in your voice. We were always available for a ball game, or whatever the guys were up to lately. And we appreciated the call.

Maybe it was time for the family to gather again for a birthday, or maybe just dinner at your place. Whatever the reason for the call, I always looked forward to hearing your voice rising from the answering machine when I pressed the button.

I wish you'd had the time to develop that Adobe Siding gag a little further, Steve. I very much wish you would call me soon with the next installment.

If there is one thing that every one of us knows and can count as a certainty, it is the fact that our voice will be stilled one day. We may view this truth with dread and denial but we know there's no escaping it. And yet there's something very cruel about a voice being stilled so suddenly as yours, at least for those of us who are left behind.

This is the sort of thing that happens to others. We read it in the newspapers every day — tragic accidents that always happen to other people — and it has always seemed so remote, as if it really hadn't happened at all. We are sad for the loss felt by others, yet it even seems somehow that those people may have been just part of an epic novel, that they may not really have existed at all — at least not in the immediate world of our existence. The mind does its best to cushion us from the harsh realities of our existence; it does little to prepare us fully for the inevitable sadnesses of life. We had no real understanding of how deeply this accident would affect us. We had no warning that such a thing might actually happen to our own family.

We have been a very lucky family. We have lost older uncles and aunts who lived to a full age and who saw their children grow and prosper. They felt their grandchildren on their knees and heard their happy voices of discovery as they found their first earthworm living in the rich soil of the garden, or saw a nest full of hatchlings emerge in a tree just outside a window. Our aunts and our uncles have always grown old with a full measure of grace, and they left behind the lessons of their lives for us to follow. They left us when they should, after a full life, rich with the experience of an accomplished generation. For our family, there was nothing to suggest that it would ever be otherwise.

But still, as we have all gotten older, I have found myself beginning to wonder which of us, which of the five siblings, would be the first to depart. It is an inevitable and immutable event that none of us can ultimately control, although there are things — like maintaining a healthy lifestyle — that we can each do to forestall it. The assumption always was, of course, that our parents would precede us in passing. This is normal and inevitable, and it is something they had also assumed would happen. The older generations are supposed to make way for the younger generations, although, in times of war and great upheaval, it is often the young who go and leave a generation of old people behind, in the silence of a landscape bereft of vibrant youthful voices, new ideas and other wonderfully foolish excitements of the young. Those are sad times, indeed, for those who survive the young. Lucky is the family whose young outlive them.

But in our family, it was not to be.

The only real preparation that we may have had for your death, and that of Janette, and young Eliot, was the early death of our cousin Phil, whose passing I still grieve to this day. Phil was in his early thirties, with the sensitivity — some might say the impracticality — of an artist. That he was talented, there is no doubt in my mind. In his work, Phil went far beyond the natural world, and I was fortunate to see many of the insightful inventions of his mind. I still miss his wry, cheerful wit and his easy laugh. I can still hear the happy sound of his voice in my mind today and I wish I could talk with him again about the nature of life, and art, and the meaning of sunlight as it first strikes a distant mountaintop in the morning. But it is too late for that. Phil is gone now, forever.

And so are you, my brother. Yet I can still hear the wonderful deep tones of your voice when I think of messages left behind on a phone answering machine, and of those many times when we walked together down that long dirt road behind your place, along the banks of the Alameda Acequia as it brings its life-giving water from an ancient river to the thirsty fields of the beautiful Rio Grande Valley. We talked of life, those many times, of the bounty of the seasons, of the kids, of travel plans for the future. The happy sound of children's voices mingled in the background with the lush sound of water rushing through spillways. Now your voice is there too — just there, in the background of my life.

And your voice will be with me always.

A Tragedy in Alaska

Part II

Bahia de Kino

Traveling South Again

September 27, 2001

It's late September now, Steve, and we've gone back to Kino Bay.

Carolyn and I remember those fine and wonderful times we had here with all of you and with the rest of the family, and we've returned to feel your presence here again. There may be others for whom these memories would be too painful; but we find a kind of peace here, away from all the meaningless distractions of daily life, yet still connected to you. I find the space and the quiet here to write these words, to tell you of a world you've left behind, to tell of all those things you've missed since you were taken away.

We pulled in to Kino Bay as the sun was setting, exhausted and relieved that we had finally returned to this quiet backwater on the Mexican coast, the place that calls us to return to simple and quiet moments by the sea. It took us four days, this time, to get here. I don't really know why, but everything seemed to conspire against our leaving Alburquerque behind for a month. Life has gotten so much more complicated this summer, and I think most of it has to do with some need we've each felt to stay just as busy as possible since your death. Some might call it avoidance or sublimation. Maybe it's the realization of our own mortality, our own brief opportunity to accomplish something with our lives. Maybe it's a powerful need for distraction so our lives are not consumed with thinking about the three of you. I know that if I allowed myself to do so, I would think almost constantly of you and Janette and Eliot. Call it whatever, but we've clearly felt a need to be more involved with the myriad issues of life than ever before.

Bahía de Kino

So I'm taking some time this morning to put down a few of the many thoughts that have passed after several days behind the wheel of our old van watching the desert world — a world you each loved so deeply — pass by our windows beyond a stream of cars and heavy-laden trucks and buses. We left town late on Tuesday evening, determined to put just a few miles behind us as quickly as possible, and we only made it to Socorro. We spent that first night in a very modest room at the San Miguel Motel. We had planned to leave Alburquerque on Tuesday morning at the latest, but there seemed to be nothing we could do to speed the process of untangling ourselves from the cobwebs of life. By the time we ran last minute errands, arranged things at the bank, and cleaned the house for our friend, Kyle, to stay in, it was well into late afternoon. And we still had to hook up that little sailboat we bought from Jon Kaplan and Joyce Wilkerson back in June — the one that Eliot and I were planning to spend time on this summer. The one that Eliot saw only once, and will never see again.

I remember a bright and curious smile on Eliot's face as he climbed aboard the little boat on its trailer parked in Jon's driveway. It was that smile of impish delight he was so well known for in his short life. It was a smile that said he now saw the possibilities for a summer of fun that a little sailboat could offer, especially a boat that was about his size. He knew how much I loved sailing, and I know he was very curious about its allure for me. And, at nine years of age, he had a powerful interest in pirates and other such scourges of the sea. A proper fascination, I thought, for a lad growing up about 900 miles from the closest ocean. A fascination I could understand.

I bought him a copy of *Treasure Island*, and I bought one for myself. I'd never actually read the book, although, like most kids, I'd seen one of the many movie versions — that old and memorable one with Wallace Beery as Long John Silver. I figured I'd better fill in that neglected part of my education to stay ahead of this particular nephew. I was surprised to find that the words "Fifteen men on a dead man's chest. Yo Ho Ho, and a bottle of rum!" apparently came from this novel. That was a good thing to know, since Eliot was now swaggering around singing those words, in the deepest voice that a nine-year-old can muster.

Carolyn and I returned to Jon and Joyce's house one evening in June to buy the boat. We came with a bottle of rum in hand, and with a bag containing four bandanas, four eyepatches, four plastic gold earrings, and four plastic cutlasses. After donning pirate regalia, I handed Jon a heavy string bag filled with one hundred of those gold Sacajewea dollars — the modern "Pieces of Eight" — and a check for the rest, and we took title to a fine little sailboat, although I hadn't yet figured out where to put her at our house. After a proper ceremony, I stuffed all the pirate regalia back into the bag and we took it home for Eliot and his cousins to amuse themselves with at some point in the near future. In fact, we had planned to see all of you just after you got back from Alaska.

After the crash, I couldn't bring myself to even deal with the little boat, so she sat in Jon's driveway for several more months. Finally, we hooked her up to the back of the van and brought her south with us to Mexico.

Fittingly, the little sailboat that Eliot and I went to see that day in Jon's driveway was a 1979 Chrysler Mutineer. I never had a chance to tell him that part, but I can imagine him and me out sailing her together, hard on the wind on a sunny afternoon with spray over the bow, and the two of us breaking into another chorus of "Fifteen men on a dead man's chest! Yo Ho Ho and a bottle of rum!"

As we finally left town, a fading sunset swept the western sky and, Steve, I know you would have paused to enjoy yet one more splash of brilliant color as it painted the edge of a cloudbank hanging just above the horizon. It was a scene each of us had experienced many times in the years we have lived in the valley of the middle Rio Grande. It was a moment that neither of us had ever grown tired of. I know you would have appreciated very much seeing a brilliant western sunset just one more time.

South of Belen, at the Mountainair/Bernardo cutoff, rugged Ladron Peak loomed alone upon the high desert off to the west, in moonlit darkness, with its many mysteries shrouded in the black of night. The name means "bandit" in Spanish, and there were lots of places for them to hide in the deep canyons and furrowed flanks of Ladron Peak. As we drove onward and southward in the night, I recalled your telling me of the time you hiked to the top with a friend, but I can't remember who it was. I always figured I could call you and ask, if it was ever that important. Now I wish I could call and ask you.

But the reason I thought about that hike was your description of arriving at the top — or at least almost at the top. I think about that tale every time I pass Ladron. There was a good reason you actually didn't get all the way to the top of Ladron that day. In fact, there might have been a few dozen good reasons on that warm Spring day. The two of you had gotten close to the very top of the mountain when you heard the unmistakable warning of a large rattlesnake, very loud and very close. It's a familiar sound to those of us who've grown up in the West, and it never fails to set the heart pumping rapidly.

Bahia de Kino

The two of you quickly backed up several steps, and took a deep breath or two, while you located the rattler. You were in the process of making a wide berth around the rattler when you ran into a second one. After you both settled down from your second heart tremor of the morning, you set a course that angled away from the second rattler. And that's when you ran into a third one. About this time, the two of you stopped to add up all of the variables regarding rattlesnakes in rocky country on a warm Spring day, and decided not to press your luck any further. There were a lot of them out there that day. They were probably very hungry and very grouchy after a long hibernation. But they had each been considerate enough to give you fair warning.

It was a beautiful day, and it was a particularly good day to leave that mountain to the rattlers. There would be another day. Maybe. Or maybe not. Come to think of it, I don't recall that you ever mentioned hiking up Ladron Peak again.

After a good night's sleep, we left Socorro in the early morning light, with the broad green valley of the Rio Grande lying to the east of us. What's left of the world's longest contiguous cottonwood forest shown brightly under the desert sun. I was reminded of the time you spent helping to start The Bosque Society. There were battles with "The Powers That Be" over leaving at least enough water in the river to support some of the original inhabitants of this valley. You felt they deserved at least a little consideration.

One day I helped you and several other people dig a deep notch through a ditchbank to place a 6" diameter pipe. It would ensure a small but constant flow of water into the beautiful oxbow that sits just below the old St. Joseph's College on that bluff overlooking the valley from the West. The water engineers had mandated a cut-off canal that starved the oxbow of water and returned it all to the river channel. This rare microcosm of river life — one of the few left along the entire river — was doomed to dry up in short order. There were fish and turtles, rare birds and plant life in this old oxbow right near the center of town. It was a precious natural resource and without your efforts, and those of a small band of other concerned people, it was doomed.

You and Rex Funk and Harvey Frauenglass and several others spent a lot of time working out some kind of arrangement with those who control the river's precious waters; and in the end, your sensible proposal won out over the engineers who had labeled irrigated fields and urban lawns as the only "beneficial use" for the water. That's a very interesting term they had developed in order to deny the sensible requests of people who tried to save a bit of water for the river and for its beautiful bosque. It left no room for those thousands, nay millions, of creatures great and small whose ancient, original claims to the water went ignored.

You managed to embellish your arguments with the appropriate amount of good-natured ridicule to expose the fraudulent arguments of engineers who saw majestic native cottonwood trees as water-wasting "phreatophites." It's another convenient and artificial term to describe the native trees, shrubs, and plants that have lived in this valley for millions of years. It also has a scientific ring to it that comes in handy for bludgeoning the well-reasoned arguments of opponents.

So you came up with the "phreato-bird," a notorious water-sucking marauder that demanded a full-scale investigation. There was even a poster of the offender to display at various hearings. It helped to point up the pseudo-scientific absurdities crafted by the water engineers.

You had a visceral understanding that the political process is only about half concerned with logical reasoning. The other half is all about showmanship; it's about circus. It's an effective way to make important points that people, and especially bureaucrats, can understand. Most people got the joke, and they quickly understood the problem better than the engineers did. They realized you can't sacrifice the long-range health of the natural world for short term gains. The long-term debt only increases.

I think that's when the tide began to turn toward more sensible solutions to our water problems in the Rio Grande Valley.

I know you would have described these events more graciously in your own way. You'd have taken a lot less credit for getting the ball rolling, and I agree that there were quite a few other people working for the changes we all knew had to happen. I realize you were not the only one involved. But I'm telling the story in my way, from my perspective — the only way I know — and so naturally I'm giving my brother most of the credit.

We stopped along I-10 at Lordsburg for lunch and then we decided to drive about two or three miles south to the old ghost town of Shakespeare. There was a locked gate across the road and a sign said the town was only open for tours on every second Saturday. We had arrived on a Wednesday, so we were out of luck. But there was a small stash of photocopied brochures in a box by the gate. There were colorful descriptions of Wild West high-jinks in this lawless town by notorious characters like Curly Bill Brocious, Billy the Kid, Russian Bill (Bill or Billy seemed to have been a popular name in those days), the Clantons, and some others you might remember from those bad western movies we watched on late night

---

Bahia de Kino

television in our youth. I sometimes wonder how these characters were regarded in their own time. It's not difficult to imagine movie-makers of the next century glorifying today's scumballs in similar fashion. Still, we should leave a place in our lives for a good yarn. We don't really need to remember all the inconveniently correct details of our history, do we?

You'll remember that broad land-locked desert valley, that *playa* the highway crosses just as you enter Arizona. After a heavy rain, shallow salt lakes stand in the flat bottom of the valley until the water soaks into the earth and replenishes some deep aquifer. The view across this vast dry valley into jagged rocky mountains is quintessentially western. It slices north into the edge of New Mexico, and it continues south into the Mexican state of Chihuahua. During springtime, the dry surface of this *playa* is swept up by afternoon winds into giant dust-storms , and visibility is cut to zero. They sweep across the highway and make driving treacherous. There was a large pileup last year and several people died, when they tried to drive through the dust. It can happen very quickly, and it's not something we can control. It's best to avoid this stretch of highway in the afternoon during springtime.

Death can come so quickly and so easily in this world. That's something I think about more often these days. In my callow youth I didn't dwell on it; but so much has changed now.

Farther into Arizona, the highway cuts through the giant boulders of Texas Canyon. I read somewhere that a lot of old western movies and TV shows were filmed here, and it figures. It's a pretty dramatic place. Although it doesn't look much like Texas.

We pass billboards advertising the notorious old town of Tombstone and the cut-off that takes you southwesterly through the grassy lands of Patagonia. We took that route when you and your family, Jimmy and Elyse, and Mom all went with us to Kino that time a few years ago for Mom's seventieth birthday. But this time we'll go west through Tucson, then we'll turn south to Nogales.

Nogales. The name means walnut trees in Spanish. The hills are covered with them, small native walnut trees filled with nuts that are half the size of the English walnuts we're used to. And they're hard as rocks. You need equipment if you want to taste one of these nuts. If you go to the trouble to crush one and then sort the tiny pieces of nutmeat out of the debris, you'll find they have all the flavor of the English variety. It just requires a lot more work, that's all. Life is hard around here; and, like most things in the desert, the *nogales* give up their treasures reluctantly.

The main crossing in downtown Nogales is a rich and surging tapestry of peoples from both sides of the border and from all parts of Mexico. It's the same at Tijuana, and Ciudad Juarez, and Ojinaga; and I imagine it's the same at every other major crossing along this border. All those people, like us, have come here following a long highway to their dreams. We're heading south to a land of grace and charm and leisure, at least for those who can afford it. Many of those waiting in the northbound lanes are looking for the opportunities that we have taken for granted all our lives and are now quite willing to forsake. In a way, each of us is trying to escape our past. To move onward to a better future. Or, in my own case, to escape the ravages of a summer of terrible memory.

We finish our paperwork at the Kilometro 21 checkpoint and then we're free, to travel south down those four lanes of highway that lead through a fertile river valley toward the towns of Imuris, Magdalena de Kino, and Santa Ana. After a stop at Santa Ana for soft drinks at a roadside restaurant, we leave the protected valley to cross the vast open desert to Hermosillo. It's a long drive through open country. There are no radio stations out here to break the long chorus of road noise. We are left to our own thoughts as we travel onward and southward.

And finally we're in Hermosillo. We stop for lunch at Sanborn's, and we visit the bookstore section where I buy that large Spanish Dictionary that I didn't buy last year, the *Diccionario de la Lengua Española*. It's the Spanish Dictionary published by the *Real Academia Española* — the Spanish Royal Academy — in 1992 in celebration of the 500th anniversary of Columbus's voyage to the New World. It gives the definitions, in Spanish, of every word I can imagine, and many I've never heard before, although a friend tells us it's not really the definitive source. It seems the *Academia* left out most of the "vulgar" words and idioms. At 1,499 Pesos ($150 US) it's an expensive purchase; but I don't gamble, smoke, buy new cars, or drink heavily, and it's a truly beautiful book that we'll enjoy for many years. And for many generations, I hope.

We make one last stop at a *supermercado* to get a few of the fresh items we'll need at our destination. The security guy in the parking lot mentions that the overcast sky is due to a distant hurricane, but that's far from our minds at this point. We load the items we bought and climb aboard for the last short stretch. And finally, we're on that last westward leg of this journey of remembrance to Bahia de Kino nestled quietly on the shore of the Sea of Cortez.

Bahia de Kino

This will be our fifth visit to Kino Bay, if memory serves. Each time we return, we feel more comfortable here.

The large south window of our rented house looks directly onto the Sea of Cortez. The constant march of waves rolls against a low sandy shore here in the protected lee of *Isla Pelicano*. Literally thousands of pelicans and other sea birds — more than we've ever seen here before — are riding the rolling surface just offshore under a hot and penetrating desert sun. I look through binoculars to scan the rolling surface and I see only a few birds that aren't pelicans — that awkward, pterodactyl-looking seabird whenever its feet touch the land. Yet they are among nature's most graceful creatures in the sky and upon the sea. I can't tell what the other birds are, and I'm sorry, Steve, because I know you would be interested in them as well. You would know what kinds of birds they are.

Birding was one of your many interests, but not an all-consuming passion. To you, it was one more rich piece of that broad canvas of life we all inhabit. Birding was another way for you to be fully involved with your surroundings, and you were amused at those who took it seriously. We joked about it now and then — such a rich vein of humor; there were nuggets lying everywhere just for the taking. Maybe one day you'd have written the *Non-Birder's Handbook of How to Get a Life*, or *Birding and Other Ailments*, amply embroidered with your wry and clever wit. I know you'd have asked for my help with editing your book, because you always thought I was smarter and more educated than you. I'm now not so sure that was the case. Now that you're gone, I've suddenly been made aware of the many things you accomplished quietly over the years, and which you never talked about.

I'd have been honored to help with that book, or with the many other books I think you could have written. I believe now that you were on the cusp of writing down some of the many things you had learned, things that would have been of great value to others. There were several books waiting, on a wide range of topics, that you never got around to writing. It's difficult to do that, and raise a couple of kids, and make dinner in the evening, and effectively run a business. I'm deeply sorry that you never had the chance to be retired — in whichever way you would have defined that term — and the freedom that it would have given to put your thoughts on paper. I am very sorry for you, and for others who would have found your work to be useful in their lives. I'm sorry I'll never read any of it now.

I Always Meant to Tell You...

I wanted you to read some of what I've been writing for these many years — but which I didn't feel was ready to show you, or anyone else but Carolyn. I didn't want you to see this stuff yet, because I didn't want you to think that maybe your older brother wasn't really such a great writer after all, that maybe I wasn't so smart after all. And now it doesn't even matter, does it?

Silver streaks break the surface of the sea outside my window. Beneath the surface, large fish are herding schools of small fish together. As each large fish lunges into the writhing mass for its catch, the surface explodes into a wave of silver as the fortunate ones take to the air to escape. And that is why so many pelicans have come to this spot this morning, to take their own advantage from the air. A pelican wheels across the sky, tucks its wings, and dives, leaving a white explosion of salt water hanging briefly in the air. It returns to the rolling surface with a beakful of living fish. After briefly riding the surface to swallow its meal, the bird lifts its wings. It takes the air again in a couple of heavy strokes to cruise high above the waves, looking, searching, for a flash of silver below the water.

They're about six inches long, these fish, and their dead carcasses litter the beach this morning, but the pelicans and the other sea birds leave the dead ones alone. Something tells them to avoid the dead ones on the shore — tells them to leave those for the vultures, and the crabs, and the flies.

Our friend Maria Pinelli, whom you'll never have the pleasure of meeting, called them *sardinas* last night when she apologized for the stench of all those little rotting bodies lying at the high water mark along this entire beautiful seven-mile stretch of white crescent beach. At six inches long, they're bigger than what we normally think of as sardines — but that's exactly what they look like: big, delicious, sardines. Maria said maybe they were part of a load that one of those fishing ships dumped at sea. Or maybe one of those ships sank in the large waves that came ashore from that hurricane that's still about 400 miles away.

I don't know how many of these beautiful silver fish were victims of this mass die-off, and I don't know how it happened; but in an area about one pace wide and three or so paces long (maybe three feet by 10 feet), I counted 64 of them. Yes, I actually counted them. Strange, isn't it, to be so preoccupied with these tiny and insignificant lives? This mass of little silver bodies now lies inert in a high-water band, mixed with seaweed and shells, that stretches the entire seven mile length of the beach. So how many are on this seven miles of beach? I don't know. I'm not sure I really care to know. I've discovered recently there are a lot of things I don't know the answers to. Many of those answers I'd rather not know.

Bahia de Kino

And the pelicans out there riding the endless, restless sea? There must be hundreds, but I don't know. I have no intention of counting them, although I tend toward that sort of trivial behavior despite the fact that I'd have no useful purpose for the information. I have always tried to think of it as a tendency toward natural scientific curiosity. I know you'd understand that.

I know that you and Janette and Eliot would each find these things very interesting. All these tiny pieces of the daily and endless dance of life and death and renewal, as it plays itself out along the sandy margins of this rich, warm, Mexican sea.

Carolyn prepared an excellent dinner of chicken breasts and sliced sauteed vegetables in canola oil over a bed of rice, and we enjoyed our first evening meal in this fine and special house with a bottle of slightly vinegary local wine — but we were too exhausted, and happy to be here, to care much about the wine. It tasted wonderful in the moment.

After dinner, we sat outside on the terraza in the darkness, facing toward an endless sea, our feet resting on the stone railing, wine glasses in our hands. We watched a brilliant moon high above our heads throw streaks of silver across a darkening sky and paint the edges of fantastic clouds bestowed by the winds of the world upon us this special evening. The endless musical rush and rumble of the sea filled the stillness and played a background to the night.

"There's a sailboat in the sky." Carolyn said softly and almost in a whisper, so as not to startle the darkness. I looked upward toward the west and I saw it — a graceful, tall-masted sloop with a long boom and a small headsail — reaching across the sky before us, racing through the night toward some distant port that no-one knows the name of. I can imagine that no-one else saw it passing silently in the night. No-one but the two of us.

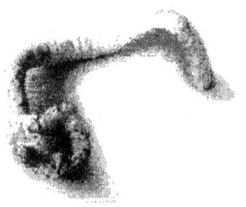

El Pargo Rojo

September 28, 2001

Dear Steve,

Our first Friday night back in Kino Bay, our second night here, we walked down to El Pargo Rojo for dinner. It's a long hike from the beautiful home that we managed to rent this year. We walked a stretch of beach that has now become familiar, into the spectacular glow of a setting sun. At our feet was a day's worth of shells, seaweed, and the other detritus left by the endless waves that wash upon this shore.

It was a melancholy journey for both of us as we retraced the steps that we had taken only two years before, with you. And with Janette, and Alec, and Eliot, our Mom, our sister Elyse, our brother-in-law Jimmie, and Alec's friend Allison.

At El Pargo Rojo, we ordered a couple of margaritas and a basket of chips with salsa. We sat for a while in familiar surroundings washed by the waning light of afternoon, each of us lost in our thoughts. We quietly toasted your memory and scooped a chipfull of fiery salsa from the bowl. We've noticed that the chips have gradually gotten less greasy in restaurants throughout Mexico, as they've discovered it's healthier, cheaper, and a lot less messy to cook them in a microwave oven instead of in a skillet of hot lard. A *telenovela* played on a TV set mounted high above a table in the front corner, but we spent our time talking and recalling the quiet beauty that pervades this little town on the sea, reliving those special times we spent here with family.

We each ordered a second margarita, followed by steaming platters of *camarrones al mojo de ajo*. Shrimp bathed in garlic butter and lying on a bed of rice, has become something of a tradition with us, and we tend to start off each of our visits this way. This year, it was a way for us to remember our dinner here with you not so long ago. But the flavor was different this time. There was something important missing — the joy of simply being here once again was leavened now by the terrible weight of memory.

The Five-Legged Band still plays at El Pargo Rojo on Fridays and Saturdays. I know you'd remember them. There are three guys in the band, and one has only one leg. Their actual name is *Los Ribereños de la Bahia*, and they've become something of a prized institution here over the years.

I requested the song, "*El fugitivo de Sonora*," which I remembered from visits in the past. And Carolyn enjoyed a softly romantic song named *"Quierame."* Drama, joy and romance, the sounds of Mexico, filled the air.

Then I requested *"De Colores."*

Carolyn studied my eyes for the tears she knew were likely to appear as the band began to sing those familiar words that you sang so well all those years with the Jug Band. The bass player saw a tear glisten down my cheek, and turned away to leave me with my thoughts. Carolyn and I held hands, listening quietly to the words, and we felt you with us there, once more.

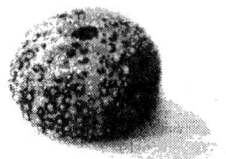

Dear Alec

September 28, 2001

Dear Alec,
    None of us knows with certainty what thoughts passed through the minds of your father, your mother, and your little brother in those last few moments before their small plane lifted from the surface of a remote lake in Alaska and crashed into a rocky hillside. This is something we can never know. We are left only with our speculations.
    Others with near-death experiences have said they thought of the strangest things in those last few moments. Things like, who will feed the cat, the rent check they were going to mail when they returned, the unpaid phone bill.
    The mind, it seems, can't really accept that the body is about to die.
    What were Steve, Janette, and Eliot thinking in their final moments? Was Steve concerned about an important meeting he was scheduled to facilitate upon his return? What of the unfinished data study that Janette was preparing for an upcoming conference on diabetes? And that final baseball practice to get ready for the Fall series — was Eliot thinking of that as their plane hurtled toward the ground? It all seems so irrelevant now. None of it matters at all, now.
    I can't be so presumptuous as to think I could read their minds in those last few moments — I don't really know what they were thinking. But I'm as sure as anything that your parents' thoughts were centered on you, Alec, and your little brother. In that final frozen moment as they stared directly into the certainty of their own mortality they were each thinking, and somehow I know this to be true, that they had just failed you both. That they were no longer able to love you and protect you as you make your prickly and uneasy way onward through the world.

Bahia de Kino

Life was destined to be difficult for you, Alec. It will be more difficult now in the wake of this tragedy, without Steve's gentle and patient touch. The family knows that. And so do you. For some reason, life for you has always been a challenge as you crash constantly into the sharp edges of a world that human society has designed, without your consent.

It's tragically ironic that your parents decided long ago to love you and protect you as best they could because they felt that you would not be in this world for long. Your life has always had a strong self-destructive focus, and they felt it was unlikely you would outlive them, or your little brother. Your father said to me once a couple of years ago.

But your father was always a bit of a worrier. I remember him fretting about me, when we were both much younger and I, too, grated against the restrictive conventions of society. I think I turned out all right, although it wasn't always easy. And now I appreciate his concern more than I did in the past.

There's a line in a popular song that makes me think of your father, my little brother. It goes, "… you were always there for me." I'm sure the writer intended it for a lost girlfriend, but now it seems so appropriate as I remember Steve. He was there whenever I logged a success, and he was quick to praise me for it. And he was gracious enough to ignore most of my failures. For some reason, his praise was always more important to me than anyone else's. We were of the same generation, and we faced many of the same battles. We each had to deal with school bullies. We each dealt with the heartbreak and confusion of dating when we came of age. And we both had to deal with a corrupt military draft system that favored those with wealthier and savvier parents than ours, those who kept their kids out of a corrupt war driven by powerful business and political interests for personal gain with no regard for the safety of a young generation. It wasn't an easy time for your father to grow up, despite what they try to tell you on television.

You're very lucky to have many good friends. We all saw how they gathered round to support you through this tragic and emotional journey. Good friends are irreplaceable.

And you're very lucky to have been born into a truly exceptional and supportive family. That always meant a lot to Steve.

Little Brothers

Consider, for a moment, the matter of little brothers. For a big brother, a younger sibling is always in the way, always wants to do something with your older friends, always wants to hang out with you. And your mother tells you to take him along. And to take care of him. We may not really appreciate them until much later in life.

Yet there's another, very tragic, younger brother problem that appears in our family — their early mortality.

As the older brother, the oldest of five, I should not be the one writing these words. I should have been the one who died first. These should be the words of my brother, or one of our three sisters. And yet, these words are mine.

But Steve, my younger brother by less than two years, is gone now.

My nephew Alec also lost a little brother in the crash that took his parents. In this way, he and I will share forever a tragic commonality.

But our family's unlucky string of little brothers goes back a few decades to the death of cousin Phil in a car accident. Phil was our cousin Gary's little brother.

And our brother-in-law Jimmie lost his younger brother several years ago in a car accident down in Texas.

I don't really know what to make of all this. Is it a coincidence? Is there something more to the story? I don't know.

I only know that the world seems suddenly a far lonelier place.

Bahia de Kino

¡Chubasco!

Bahia de Kino
September 29-30, 2001

SATURDAY MORNING

The sea is rough this morning, much rougher than it usually is in the morning in this protected bay where a normally very quiet part of the ocean washes against the edge of the world. Usually, the onshore winds will have died during the night and the morning sea will gently kiss this shore with a six-inch surf, as a blazing yellow sun rises in the east and casts its rays across a pattern of small bird tracks left on wet sand.

But last night and this morning the surf stays strong against the shore, and there is a northward set to it. And it had been awfully hot last night. The sea and the air are telling us something this morning, our second morning here, and we're not yet sure of the message. We arrived late Thursday, needful of the peace and quiet we've come to expect from our previous visits here; but this morning it looked as if our quiet refuge would elude us for a little while longer.

In the sky, far to the south and east, there are clouds this morning, a dense bank of clouds that clings heavily to the horizon. We remember a friendly parking lot attendant in Hermosillo who told us there was a hurricane about 400 miles offshore and that's where the clouds are coming from. He mentioned the clouds because the desert sun of summer and fall is normally a merciless red eye glaring down upon the residents of Hermosillo. There's rarely any significant cloud cover for relief. To us, those few high cirrus clouds drifting above were of no consequence. To him, they were unusual and worth noting.

The customary strong afternoon winds of yesterday had sent their ranks of whitecaps running to the land. They died in the night, and there was no wind left this morning to drive the sea onto the shore. Yet, we hear it in a windless dawn, pounding and churning the long sandy beach outside our window. And sounding as if it might enter the house, if it chose to. Sounds in the night can do that to you; they can be stronger in the mind than they really are.

Distant winds circling the hurricane have sent these remnants of a furious ocean to our shore to dissipate their energy. There is very little heat on the land because of the heavy cloud cover, so there's little temperature differential to drive the daily onshore winds; today, the clouds have kept the sun-driven heat engine at bay. Still, waves are pounding against the shore. In the distance we can see the dense forward edge of a rounded cloud bank as it passes onward and northward from far beyond the Baja Peninsula.

Will it turn? Could it come our way? That sort of thing has been known to happen. Hurricanes are notoriously unpredictable. People here still talk of that hurricane a few years back, the one that came up the Sea of Cortez and pounded the shore here at Bahia de Kino. That's the incalculable force that dredges tons of sand from the bottom and creates wide beautiful beaches, like the one just outside our window. It can happen here; and it does happen, now and then.

This hurricane seems much closer to us now than it should be, according to the predictions. For now, there's but to wait and see what happens. In the meantime, we'll listen to the surf. And to the light, unsettled wind. I decide to keep a log of this singular experience, our first hurricane, on my reliable Mac laptop.

SATURDAY AFTERNOON

In the late afternoon, I take a swim.

I dive into the faces of the strengthening waves, and rise behind the crests to watch them as they crash onward to the shore. A broad field of white foam edges the entire coastline. I look southeasterly toward Isla Pelicano, lying like a huge grounded ship in the shallows, and I see a dark roll of cloud that seems to be curving around the island yet high above it. Soon it passes over me, standing in awe in the surf below.

I call to Carolyn and we watch this strange cloud push onward across the sky. After dinner, we sit together on the terraza and watch the heavy surf with dark clouds above it.

Lightning crashes closer and closer from deep in the black heart of the storm as it stands offshore waiting for night to mask its landfall. The surf roars angrily against the shore throughout this long night. We sleep fitfully, and awaken often to the sound of heavy surf, as we await the storm's next move.

SUNDAY MORNING

In the morning, the wind has backed and is now coming from the shore side of the house, pushing heavily against the two glass front doors. Heavy rain pours from two roof canales into the concrete entry court. Rivulets of rain drive through the court and sluice beneath the doors. The fronds of tall palms that line the road and shade the courtyard slash wildly through the air. The windows rattle against each sudden burst of wind.

Heavy rain flattens the ocean. Strong gusts peel that leading knife edge off the waves just before they crash, and the wind sends it flying upward into the sky like a lace curtain flying from a window. In the distant grey spume, Mexican shrimp fishermen call to one another by radio. We watched late last night as their lights disappeared, one by one, in a descending wall of wind-blown mist. This morning they still ride hard against the wind and wave. They left port last night expecting the hurricane to continue northward in the open ocean, but it veered toward the east and crossed the Baja Peninsula into the Sea of Cortez. Risk-taking is common among fishermen, and so is death. Now they radio messages to one another, discussing the damage, comparing conditions, the sea state, the wind. Our rented house, like many along this coast, has a VHF radio on the wall; and we listen to their crackling voices, in serious, rapid Spanish, as the wind pounds against the house.

> "Are you OK?"
> "Have you heard from El Condor?"
> "How long will it last?"
> "¿Quien sabe?"

Carolyn walks down to the nearby *tiendita*, Super Juliana, which is about a block away, to see if they have any Hermosillo newspapers left. The wind is fierce outside the courtyard gate, and she pulls her jacket tightly as she leaves. No, there are no papers at all today, because of the storm. The latest word is that the storm has hit San Carlos hard and is heading our way. Earlier, it slammed directly into the Baja Peninsula, and there are many deaths reported.

The ceiling fan turns slowly overhead. So far, we still have electricity. Outside my window, a large perfect wave curls upward and forward; its face grows darker in the shadow of the overhanging edge as it sits frozen for a brief moment. The wind peels that thin leading edge and flings it skyward just before

---

Bahia de Kino

the entire face crashes forward into the swirling surf. The crisp and clean sound of impact booms into the walls of the house. It rattles the glass in the windows. It shakes the floor.

¡Hay cuatro muertos! ¡Es muy peligroso!

The radio crashes through the sound of wind and wave with bad news for the little fishing community just down the coast. Maybe they're talking of the situation in the Baja, and maybe not. We have no idea how much of this is fact, and how much is rumor. Reception is inconsistent and sometimes scratchy. Tomorrow they may mourn their dead, as they have so many times in the past. As fishing villages have always done.

Several shrimp boats are riding at anchor now in the lee of the island. We can barely see them through the heavy mist.

¡... en veinte minutos... con mucha velocidad...!

The radio transmission is breaking up now. And suddenly the island is gone, completely wrapped in the fury of the storm. In twenty minutes, the leading wall of the storm will hit us. All we've seen so far were the preliminaries. The waves are larger now, maybe five to six feet high, and the tide is coming in.

A piece of Styrofoam trash skitters crazily down the beach. An empty aluminum can chases after it.

The island reappears for a moment and then disappears again. The radio crackles. It's a woman's voice calling to her husband's boat. We've heard her voice before. She's been calling all morning. She gets no answer.

The waves grow still larger, each with a heavy cargo of dirty sand ripped from the ocean's floor. The wind sweeps across the sea parallel to the shore and tears the tops off waves for as far as we can see through the flying mist. High tide has finally come. Waves wash across the entire beach and slosh against the houses.

Nature will often remove all traces of human arrogance and will redesign her beaches at will. Now that high tide has arrived, we're lucky that the winds are parallel to the beach. We can only hope that when the following wall of this vast circular storm comes ashore, the tide will be down. If it isn't, we'll take a pounding from the ocean.

SUNDAY AFTERNOON

We feel each gust of this wall of wind as it shakes the house, and we hear an occasional screech here and there which we can't identify. We lost power sometime a while back, and the radio went silent. It's about 1:12 in the afternoon. There's a good battery in this little Mac laptop so I can still record my impressions. And I'm glad for daylight so I can hunt and peck my way around the keyboard.

We hear a loud ripping sound as a cobbled-together plywood cover is torn off the Hotel Saro about three houses to the east of us. The ripped pieces of old plywood are out there wallowing drunkenly around in the surf now, waiting for the winds to turn so they can fulfill their destiny as lethal flying projectiles. With any luck, the churning ocean will dig deep graves for them on the beach.

We watch as the front door bulges inward against the wind, and we realize there is only a very small piece of wood holding the strike plate. We lock the dead bolt as well and roll a large ceramic plant holder in front of the door, with a pillow to cushion it. The door still bulges inward at the top with each screaming gust of wind, and water leaks down the wall above it where the wind has forced it under the porch roof tiles. We're lucky the tiles seem to be well fastened and the porch structure is sound.

We have pulled all the plastic furniture off the beachside *terraza* and put it into the spare bedroom, so it doesn't start flying around when the wind turns. And then we realize we can't lower that main heavy vinyl rolling cover — the one that lowers to protect the wide seaward sliding glass doors in a hurricane. There's no power to operate the electric motor. One look at those big glass doors tells us there's no way they'll stand up to the heavy wind pressure of a hurricane.

Sometimes these modern conveniences can be our worst enemies. Why does every damn thing have to be electrified, anyway? There's a lot to be said for allowing a little manual labor in the world, or at least a manual override — especially when there's a goddam hurricane coming. If there is a manual override somewhere on this vinyl protective cover, it certainly isn't apparent to us.

If the power is miraculously restored, we'll lower that heavy vinyl cover as quickly as possible, then just crawl out the bedroom window if we need to be on the terraza for any reason. But we don't expect anyone to go out in this storm any time soon to repair the power lines that are probably lying somewhere out there on the ground and crackling wildly in the howling rain.

So we craft a plan. When the wind turns, we'll move all the living room furniture as far out of the way as we can and we'll wedge the front and back doors

---

Bahia de Kino

open with large potted plants. Then we'll stand back and watch what happens. We figure it's easier to clean up some sand and water than it is to get a bunch of broken doors and windows repaired in a remote Mexican beach town. While we would find the process culturally interesting, that's not the reason we came down here, and we can't afford to spend a lot of time doing that now. After the storm, we'll clean things up and continue with our vacation — another in a long string of very interesting vacations we've had over the years.

Outside, we hear the powerful sucking sound of water as each departing wave rips tons of sand from the beach and hands it to the next advancing wave to send crashing back to the shore. There's a momentary quiet as the front of the next wave hovers in the air. And then we hear the crash as it falls, and an explosion of dirty water shoots high into the air, the impact rattling the windows, the doors, and the very foundations of the house.

In good weather, Kino Bay is a long and beautiful seven-mile crescent shape that faces about due south at the center. We happened to get lucky this year and rented a very nice home located toward the eastern end of the bay, generally under the lee of Isla Pelicano. This may be something of a fine point under normal circumstances, but today there are reasons it could be important. A hurricane requires three elements to build huge waves that can destroy houses and the like. It needs a high wind speed, long wind duration, and something sailors call 'fetch.' This last term simply means it requires a broad stretch of open ocean for waves to build to monstrous proportions.

Although Isla Pelicano lies several miles offshore, it effectively blocks the most massive and destructive waves from forming at this end of the bay if the wind comes from the south. The island gives us some protection from that long tongue of ocean that extends southward, and ultimately, to the open Pacific Ocean. In fact, even the narrowness of the Sea of Cortez itself can help prevent huge waves from forming, as long as the wind is blowing eastward or westward across the sea — and not from the south, directly up that long open throat of the sea. That's how the theory goes.

At some point it occurs to us that the same wind that is paralleling our stretch of this long crescent-shaped beach is blowing almost straight onto the beach as it curves outward at the western end. We grab our binoculars to look at that end, but the surf-spray mostly blocks our view. We can only hope they're not suffering major damage down there.

We discuss spelling each other off to allow us each some nap time, because sooner or later — maybe even very late tonight — things around here could start to get nasty. But neither of us shows the least inclination to take a nap. There's just too much to see and experience here, in our first hurricane.

We decide to put together an "abandon ship bag" — that's our sailing influence coming into play — with the essentials we'll need if the house goes in the storm: our passports, car keys, wallets, money, sleeping bags, our laptops with impressions of our interesting vacation so far. We realize we have no communication now with the outside world, and we have no idea where this storm is heading from here. We forgot to bring that little battery-powered radio we've had with us on other trips, but there appears to be no radio reception at this house anyway. Last year we tuned in daily to that excellent station at the Universidad de Sonora in Hermosillo, but this year we aren't able to get them. So far we haven't felt like going out to sit in the van and listen for news, in case that radio is working better than the one in the house. What difference could it make, anyway? I'm not sure we would leave here now even if we knew more about the direction this storm is heading. We're probably safer here than on slippery roads with a lot of panicked people driving badly. Still, if push comes to shove, we'll be ready to leave with our emergency kit bag in hand.

And the seabirds? What of the pelicans, the gulls, the others? They're still out there, riding the air, or riding the crests of the ocean as if nothing unusual is happening. I see several flights heading almost directly, and almost effortlessly, into the wind. And then I see them return down the coast fishing, always fishing, here at their eternal home. One spots a fish near the surface, dives for it, and then comes up to ride the roiling surface. They seem little concerned at an event that strikes terror into the hearts of most of us. To them, it's another day at the beach. Life goes on, as usual.

The seaspray lifts just a little, and we spot four shrimp draggers out there riding large waves in the lee of Pelican Island. Their bows are riding high into the air before plunging into the trough in a spray of water, then lifting again to the next crest. They look awfully damned uncomfortable out there, but safe. There's another boat much farther to the west, fighting its way toward the island. As we watch, it turns broadside to the waves in a gust and it wallows in the trough, then it slowly turns back upwind and into the storm. We can see that they still have their nets out and we guess they're using them to dampen the roll of their boat in

---

Bahia de Kino

the heavy water. Since we have no power, we no longer hear them talking on the VHF to each other and to their families at home. We wonder how they're doing out there, and hope they haven't lost any crew to the churning sea.

The wind now has begun to turn and to sweep across the *terraza*. Unfortunately, the tide is still very high and water sweeps constantly against the foundations as it spills over the low sea wall at the crest of each wave. It's about 2:30 in the afternoon, Sonora time.

Just outside this house, beyond a thin sheet of plate glass, the usually placid Sea of Cortez has become a gray and angry ocean, covered as far as the eye can see with large wind-sculpted crests of foam. There are times, usually when the weather is warm and benign, when humans plant their homes into the very margins of the sea, despite strong evidence that the sea returns remorselessly now and then to the very place they've chosen to build. And there are times, like this one in fact, when Mother Nature chooses to stuff a good measure of human arrogance back down our whimpering throats.

And if we have no power tonight? That's very likely. Even in good weather, the power often fails here. Every home along this coast keeps a supply of candles ready. But we may not have power restored for several days after an event like this. And what do we do then? What, can two healthy people find to do in a romantic tropical climate in the dark? The fact is, we'll be far too exhausted tonight for anything but sleep.

It's about 3:30 in the afternoon now, and the winds seem to have moderated for some reason. In the sky to the east, over beyond the old fishing village of Bahia de Kino Viejo, we see a patch of blue sky with a few clouds in it. Does it mean we're nearly through the storm? Or is it only the eye of this huge monster? The sky straight to the south of us still carries a heavy cargo of black cloud. If the eye of the storm is passing just to the east of us, we might dodge the bullet again. The wind might parallel the beach in the opposite direction when that next wall of the storm hits. But if the eye passes directly over us, the next wind could be straight onto the shore. The tide is still very high now. The waves are still washing up against the homes along here. For now, the winds have grown strangely quiet, and we wait.

We are now in what we assume is the eye of the hurricane, and we decide to walk down the street looking for someone who might actually know what's going on with this storm. Saro is gone, maybe to visit friends in a safer place like Hermosillo. The *tiendita* Super Juliana, across the street from Saro's, is *cerrado*. At the next *tiendita*, Abarrotes Lupita, there is a nice young man sitting on a crate and reading an old newspaper. He doesn't really know much about the storm, as far as we can tell. And, while he's friendly, he just doesn't really seem to care much about all this either. We walk back to the house, get in the van, and drive off to look for Maria, our contact here who rented us the house.

As we're driving along, we pass several police and fire vehicles, and no one in or around them appears to be concerned, either. The thought occurs that if we were in mortal danger, they would probably be going door to door to warn us all to evacuate. But this is Mexico and, like much of the rest of the world, Mexicans tend to think that we Americans always make a big deal out of everything. Down here they expect people to take care of themselves without always calling for help; and most Mexicans would be embarrassed to do so.

Maria isn't at home, so we stop across the street at the Restaurant Pargo Rojo. There are some cars parked in the lot, nosed up to the building. Inside, people are enjoying a nice candlelight dinner in the dim light of an overcast afternoon, as if there's little in the world to bother them. Every restaurant here keeps a supply of candles ready for such a situation. A young waiter tells us that this is indeed the eye of the hurricane and that the other half is due to make landfall about 5:00 p.m. Yes, this is the hurricane that was supposed to stay far out in the Pacific and go north to dissipate over colder water, but it turned to the northeast instead, and it hit the Baja hard before coming directly over us. The second half is supposed to be stronger than the first. After bidding *¡buena suerte!* to the restaurant staff and customers, we go back to our rented home to prepare for the second wall of this storm.

First we move everything out of the living room, in case those big glass doors start to look like they might blow out when the wind comes straight in off the water. We check for a safety glass sticker in the corners of the windows, but we find none. We make the final decision that if the wind really gets strong and dangerous, we'll open the front and back doors and let it blow on through. Cleaning up a wet, dirty floor beats dealing with all the flying shrapnel generated by shattered glass doors. We also put all the stuff we want to take with us in a pile just inside the bedroom door.

Then there is little to do but relax – an unlikely possibility – and wait. We decide this is a very good time for some dinner.

Carolyn lights the stove with one of those little butane flame-throwers we bought in Nogales, and she puts together a hearty potato soup. We pour a couple of glasses of nice red Mexican wine, cut slices off a large loaf of bread, and eat our

Bahia de Kino

dinner while we wait. There's almost no wind, but we listen to a roaring sea still pounding the shore just outside those large open glass doors.

After dinner, we take our wine glasses and a couple of plastic chairs onto the terraza. We have decided to enjoy our first hurricane in elegance and style. We sit back and relax in the approaching night, and we watch as the center, the eye, the oculus of the storm swings back to the right and stays almost due south of us. An arm of the storm sweeps across us and throws gusts of wind and rain across the terraza. We step quickly back into the house.

The gust passes, and we wait for the storm to make landfall. It is now about 6:00 p.m., and the second wall of the storm is late arriving. It seems to have stopped moving forward while it regroups its forces. The sea is still roaring, but the tide is now receding and the eye appears to be widening just a little. We return to our chairs on the terraza to study this evolving phenomenon. By 7:00 p.m., we wonder if maybe the storm has stalled right over us and might hit later in the night. By 8:00 p.m., in the waning light of the day, we notice that the storm has actually ceased its massive rotation; this gigantic wheel in the sky has stopped turning, its clouds and its winds having been snagged on the mountains that line both sides of the narrow Sea of Cortez.

As far ar we can tell, it's actually breaking up right before our eyes.

This hurricane is being dismembered, as we watch, by the coastal mountains of Mexico. It's splitting apart into a collection of heavy gray thunderstorms adrift in an overcast sky. The sky grows darker with the night. Somewhere on the other side of this dense cloud covering lies the moon, almost full now, and it fills the sky with a soft glow of light. Other than lights on some of the fishing boats riding to their anchors east of Isla Pelicano, it's the only light visible, and it illuminates the pieces of the storm as it breaks apart before our eyes.

Over the next several days, this massive bank of heavy clouds will drift far inland across the desert and deliver its cargo of water back to the land from whence it came. From Kino Bay, it will travel to the northeast and its rain will quench the deserts. Then it will move onward to those rich lands of the midwestern US, and it will fill the mighty rivers that flow once again to the sea.

We go to bed very late after watching the wind subside, its energy still deep within the pounding sea. The waves will crash onto the shore all through the night. Sometime in the night, I hear the sound of a refrigerator motor running and I feel a breath of cooling air from the ceiling fans above our bed.

MONDAY MORNING

Outside, the faintest light of an overcast dawn has entered our window. My watch on the bedside table says it's 5:45 in the morning. I roll over to hug Carolyn, and I whisper softly in her ear, "We survived our first hurricane, Dear." She giggles at the absurdity of the remark.

The sea is calmer this morning, although the energy of the previous day is still evident upon its rolling surface. The persistent roar has now become a quiet suss and moan as it gently caresses the shore — almost in apology for its rough behavior of the day before. One of the shrimp trawlers lies hard aground, canted over, on a long sand spit that extends eastward from Isla Pelicano — a sand spit created by other hurricanes over the centuries. Several men are in the shallow water, inspecting for damage, attaching heavy lines so they can pull the boat off the sand this afternoon when the tide returns. Then they'll tow it to shore for repairs, or maybe all the way south to the yards at Guaymas if the damage is bad enough.

We hail Alfredo, one of our Mexican friends, as he walks along the beach and we ask him the name of this storm.

"Julieta." he says.

"Pues, un beso de Julieta." I say in return.

He laughs and adds, *"¡Un beso salvaje de Julieta!"*

A savage kiss indeed, from Hurricane Juliette.

Finally Juliette has passed. The Sea of Cortez is calm once more. And I can return to the difficult task of writing about my brother.

AFTERWORD:

On Monday, October 1, 2001, the Hermosillo newspaper, *El Imparcial,* was again available in Kino Bay. The headline read, *"Azota 'Julieta' Sonora"* — "Juliette Lashes Sonora." According to initial published accounts there were six deaths of Mexican citizens caused by hurricane Juliette as she stormed her way through the State of Sonora, and many more in Baja California, which was hit by the full force of her violent winds and waves.

The deaths were supposed to have occurred on a tourist yacht named Poseidon that was reported sunk offshore halfway between Guaymas and Bahia de Kino, north of Isla San Pedro Nolasco, with 11 US tourists and six crew

---

Bahia de Kino

members aboard. The accounts mentioned no survivors or wreckage found as yet, and all were presumed lost at the time. But later accounts said it was a "dive boat" with a load of scuba divers and they all donned their wetsuits when they realized the boat was doomed. They bobbed around in the warm waters of the Sea of Cortez until they were found and rescued safely a day or so later.

There was massive flooding from Juliette's torrential rains, with much damage and many left homeless in the southern part of Sonora just below Guaymas. A number of bridges, roads and highways were washed out at various locations.

The shrimp boat that was beached on the island was pulled off the sand a day or so after the storm passed, and we were told that it sustained little damage. There were no reported losses in the fishing fleet.

We had no way of knowing it at the time, of course, but Juliette dropped from actual hurricane status as she passed over the mountains of the Baja Peninsula, and her winds decreased to 70 miles per hour. She was considered to be a violent tropical storm when she reached Kino Bay and threatened to push our front door in. Over the days that followed, and as she proceeded inland, it was reported that her welcome rains replenished many of the dry reservoirs of drought-wracked northern Sonora.

Dear Eliot

October 2, 2001

Dear Eliot,

 I wish I could remember all the moments we spent together in your brief life. At your young and callow age, you would likely think I was being too maudlin; but I need these memories now more than you do. Youth is a time of infinite possibility and careless whim. As we grow older, we begin to see the very real ends of possibility, and we begin to realize our limits. In the end, we are left only with the flickering memories of success and failure to embroider the edges of our lives. It's both the privilege and the burden of an older generation to hoard, and to need, these fragments and shards of the past. It's our personal archeology, meaningless to others, meaningful only to ourselves. We look again for that bright flame of hope in the next generation.

 I was talking with your good buddy Peter Dever just the other day. He spoke of needing to spend a long and punishing day of hiking and rock climbing in the Juan Tabo area of the foothills. I was reminded of the last time I went hiking in the Juan Tabo with you. So many things remind me of you these days.

 It was a bright chilly and windy day in the early Spring. You were very young then, maybe five or six years old. The four of us, you and me, your brother Alec, and your Dad, were taking a short afternoon hike through the foothill scrub oak and boulder country. You complained at first about how difficult it was to keep up with the rest of us, with your short legs; but then you managed somehow. Especially since the other three of us wasted little time listening to your carping. Soon you fell into stride and stayed with us as we walked by large granite boulders, piñon, cactus and oak. The little creek was running, ice cold, full of snow

---

Bahia de Kino

melt, rushing impatiently down the face of the mountain to disappear into the broad alluvial plain below.

Your Dad and I walked ahead, savoring the crystal clarity of afternoon sunlight as it lay upon a high desert diorama of rugged plant life thriving among giant pieces of mountain. You and Alec engaged in the usual big brother/little brother taunts and torments. Alec whacked you with a tree branch. You complained to your Dad and me, and we mostly pretended to ignore the whole thing as we kept an eye out to make sure nothing very serious happened. Then you whacked Alec with something or other and he chased you down. It's what brothers do. It's what your Dad and I did when we were kids. Those are the rules of the game of life. The ancient rules that predate every one of us. We all play by the ancient rules.

As we crossed the creek, Alec kicked cold water on you and you cried out in surprise, "Dad! Uncle Perry! Alec kicked cold water on me!"

I turned and walked back to investigate the scene of the crime. You stood there with a weepy face.

"He kicked cold water on you?" I asked, looking very concerned.

"Yeah, Alec kicked cold water on me!" you answered.

"You mean like this?" I asked and kicked another spray of cold water on you.

Your jaw dropped, stunned for just a moment, before that familiar determined look, and ready laugh, returned to your sparkling eyes. You pursed your lips and yelled, "No, like this!" And you kicked cold water all over me.

"Oh!" I said, "You mean like this?" And I kicked another wall of icy spray as you ran to dodge it.

This continued until we were both drenched and cold and looking very ridiculous, then we all hurried back to the car to warm up and head for home. It was another lesson for a young boy: never trust an uncle around cold water.

Water is the essence, the very stuff of life. It's the stuff of human communion. And it's probably the simplest and most versatile toy ever conceived. The possibilities are endless.

Aunt Carolyn and I drove cross-country in the middle of a hot summer to the Family Reunion that occurs every other year at Barren River State Park in southern Kentucky. Your family had arrived a few days earlier.

It was late in the afternoon when we pulled into the parking lot and checked into our room. I immediately pulled on my swim trunks and headed for the pool. Your Dad had just fetched you out of the pool after a long day in the water. He'd taken you and Alec to change into some dry clothes before dinner. When

I surfaced from a long underwater glide, I saw you and your Dad walking by in your clean, dry clothes. When you saw me in the water you stopped with a broad smile, and stood at the edge of the pool.

"Eliot!" I cried out. "How've you been? How was your trip? Are you having fun here in Kentucky?" My right hand reached out, dripping with water, to shake yours.

You reached to grab my hand as a brief look of suspicion crossed your Dad's face. He knew his older brother very well, and he sensed mischief in the air, like when an uncle says, "Quick! Pull my finger!" That one's so old, I think cavemen invented it. Fortunately, at least from my perspective, your father was a bit too late to prevent what he saw coming. You reached for a hearty handshake, and then an uncontrollable urge came over me. It was like that moment when someone asks a question that just hangs in the air as perhaps the best "straight line" you'll ever get. You go ahead and make the wisecrack, without thinking of the consequences, because you know you'll never get another opportunity like this one.

As soon as you grasped my hand, I pulled you from the dry concrete apron of the pool, over my head, and face first into the water. You came up sputtering and protesting, and stating the painfully obvious: "These were my dry clothes, Uncle Perry!"

I said something like, "Not anymore they're not!" You laughed at the joke and splashed water back at me, and we engaged in a short water fight. Then I lifted you out of the pool and into the waiting arms of your exasperated father as he rolled his eyes. The two of you trudged back to your room to change clothes, again.

In my particular world view, it was the sort of foolishness that uncles and nephews were created to enjoy. It's the sort of mischief I knew you'd inflict on sons and nephews of your own some day.

Something there is about water that always reminds me of you, Eliot. Like any young kid, you were fascinated with the stuff. It's a fascination I have always shared with my nieces and nephews, and I hope I never live to outgrow it. I don't really believe in heaven and all that business, but not a day passes without me hoping somehow we'll meet again, my young friend. Somehow in a special place where there's water enough to enjoy forever. Enough for you and me to kick cold water at each other again till we're both exhausted. A place where I can pull you headfirst into the pool again.

Bahia de Kino

After Hurricane Juliette

October 2, 2001

It's Tuesday now, Steve.

I glanced at the Hermosillo newspaper and that's how I knew it was Tuesday, although I think I'd rather forget what day, what month, even what year it is. There are more important things in life, aren't there? Especially this year. This terrible year.

The sea is calm once again, and the sun came out this afternoon. We have electrical power now, as I told you, but we still don't have water at the taps. We have no idea what the problem is and we haven't spent much time asking about it since everyone has their particular theory, but nobody here really knows why we have no water. This is our second day without tap water, but it's not really a big problem.

We bathed in the sea this morning. The sky was overcast as the remains of Juliette slowly move inland, and the ocean is just a bit cooler than it had been. The cool water had a cleansing edge to it that peeled days of anxiety from our souls as we dove into small curling waves and felt the water flow again over our bodies. It was almost magical to bathe once more in this warm ocean, in this desert backwater to the world.

We have several jugs of drinking water, and we go to the sea when we need a bucket of water to flush the toilet. We're living very well, in fact, and we're more in touch with the requirements of our environment. Even with this small inconvenience, we're living a better life than shore-dwelling people did for centuries. Being without running water for awhile doesn't really matter much to us. We have a good supply of excellent books to read, I have writing materials, and Carolyn has everything she needs to draw beautiful pictures of the sea, the

---

Bahia de Kino

land, Mexico. Life is good for us and there is little else we really need here in Kino Bay.

Bahia de Kino is not really so remote that society couldn't easily distract us, if we allowed it. But we made the choice not to ask for cable TV in this house, or a phone, or any other of the daily inanities to which America seems hopelessly addicted. And it's unlikely anyone will bother us here if it isn't terribly important. Even then, they'll probably have a hard time finding us. I very much needed to lose myself here for awhile at the end of this summer, in the remainder of what's left of my own life.

This has been a terrible summer for all those who loved each of you, and I wish I could go back several months to stop these things from happening. As your big brother, I should have done something to protect you.

The hurricane that just left us caused a lot of damage near here and on the Baja Peninsula. It destroyed the homes, really the shanties, of many poor people who lost everything in the heavy flooding that swept through in its wake. They're the desperate ones who eke out a living on the margins of an avaricious society. They're the ones who get hit the hardest each time this happens. They have the least to lose, by society's distorted standards, and yet they always lose the most. The destruction that occurred throughout the State of Sonora was well covered by the Hermosillo newspaper, and some hard questions were asked about whether local governments could have done more to lessen the damage. It was a big story that was covered for several days by the local paper, yet was barely mentioned in the Tucson rag that's available here for the large number of Arizona residents with beach homes in Kino. Americans don't seem to care much about their immediate neighbors to the south.

I'm very sorry for the many people who lost family members in the World Trade Center attack in early September, and in a strange way I'm glad you didn't have to see it, Steve. It was horrific and I was as stunned as anyone else, although I was not as surprised as most people were that many of the abuses our economic system has visited upon other peoples in the name of "the bottom line" have come back to us, to rest upon once-sacred American soil. It's clear we're no longer exempt from the bitter wrath of those who have lost loved ones in secret US-sponsored massacres in remote jungles and villages throughout the world. Those who died in the World Trade Center were the victims of a national machinery driven by avarice and gone terribly wrong.

I Always Meant to Tell You...

Studs Terkel once described "the bottom line" as one of the most terrible terms we have ever invented because it's completely impersonal and amoral, and it justifies any means we use to accomplish it. Still, it wasn't "people who hate freedom" who planned the astounding attack seen by thousands of New Yorkers on their way to work that morning, and by millions around the world. It wasn't a small cadre of "enemies of peace-loving people everywhere" that clearly targeted the American business community who make billions exploiting the third world and who also targeted their protectors in the Pentagon. And yet, the spin is that this was an attack only on ordinary Americans.

If the CIA had managed to pull off something like this in one of the countries we currently designate as unfriendly, there would be "plausible deniability" and justifications given at the very highest levels of our government — and opprobrium would be heard from only a few brave souls in high office. Commendations would quietly be given to those who lurk in secret offices behind closed doors. And the business of America would go on as usual. How many more times will this happen before we demand a measure of justice and equity and fairness in our dealings with the world? I'm very sorry to say this, Steve, but I'm not optimistic.

I know this "leftist" wrath always troubled you, Steve, yet deep in your soul you harbored similar high moral standards — and you were always outraged at blatant injustice and racism. But you picked your battles carefully, and you thought before you spoke. And when you spoke, your words carried the weight of reason. You preferred to lead by example, and your life was your message, eloquently delivered.

I remember times when I spoke too long and too hard about an unjust system. Your eyes quietly suggested that maybe I'd gone a little too far, that I'd already made my point. You were right, but it hadn't yet quelled the outrage I felt, the feelings of guilt at my own complicity in our nation's crimes against humanity, at my inability to speak of it more clearly.

But why bring that up at this time? What's the point of it, anyway? You've heard this before and there's no reason to get into it again. So why speak of it now?

Because you've gone from me forever now, and there's no way in hell I'll ever share these thoughts with you again. It's exhausting being in this moment and wishing you were here now, you and Janette and Eliot, so we could walk this beach again, and talk once more over the gentle sound of waves lapping the shore.

Yet I must confess something to you now, something born completely of my own selfish needs:

Bahia de Kino

If I were given the power to reverse only one of the tragic events of this year, without hesitation I would stop that small plane you were in from crashing in the back country of Alaska. I would choose to stop the accident that took you, Janette, and Eliot from our lives and I'd sacrifice the others.

And to save you the guilt, I would never tell you the choice was mine.

I Always Meant to Tell You...

My Best Friend

October 10, 2001

Suddenly life has become much more a burden, Steve.

I'm very much looking forward to the day when I don't really have to give a damn what day it is. You always knew that about me — that I wanted the freedom not to care about the norms of society. But I could never afford that luxury. And neither could you, of course. But you never had that consuming drive to leave it all behind and start off again somewhere else. To surface in a place where nobody knows your name, or your past. Your occasional successes. Your many failures.

Failure was never a companion of yours. Life for you wasn't always easy and gracious, but you made the best of it. Most people would count my life to have been fairly successful, yet I just feel there's so much more I could have done with the years I've seen pass before my eyes.

I know it's the conventional wisdom that you can't run away from problems. That they follow you everywhere you go. That the problems are within you. I know that's what you always thought. I knew your moods and your expressions for all your life, Steve. I've known them for 54 years now. I can still see them in your eyes, even now.

But, like so much of conventional wisdom, I think that's a load of bull that society's been peddling for a long time to keep people's noses to their work. And that's also exactly what you knew I'd say, isn't it?

Think about it for a moment, Steve. If it were true, why do so many people move away from childhood homes and find challenging careers and relationships that could never have been possible were they saddled with the history of childhood and family. To your family, you're always the same kid you were when you did something very stupid, when you wrecked that new bike, or that car you

---

Bahia de Kino

finally bought on your measly salary as a fry cook or a hospital orderly. When you move far away, you can reinvent yourself entirely — and people will believe your story, if it's not outrageous. There's not going to be anybody to dispute it. Think about it, Steve, and you'll know I'm right.

So why didn't you and I ever leave for parts unknown? Why have we lived all our adult lives close to family, although we've broken ties to most of our childhood friends? Why did neither of us ever escape our past? We had our reasons, and they were different for each of us. But, what were they?

I remember a 1960s movie called "Woman in the Dunes." This guy is imprisoned with a woman in a house located in a deep depression in the dunes. They have to keep removing the sand that daily threatens to bury them. Guards send food down in a basket, but the man and woman cannot escape up the constantly collapsing banks of sand. Then one day, the guards take her away for a medical reason and they forget to pull the basket up. He tests the basket and he pulls himself to freedom. But at the top he sees a changed and frightening world... and he lowers himself back into the safety of his eternal prison.

There are reasons neither of us left, aren't there, Steve? I think I know most of my own reasons now, although it's not likely I'll ever really understand them. And now I believe that it's really not necessary that I do understand them. It's very possible that a full understanding of the choices we've each made isn't necessarily a good thing.

And I think I know some of your deepest underlying reasons too, although I could never know them all. They lie hidden forever now behind that famously Sphinx-like expression of yours. It's obviously one of the frustrations of my life, or I wouldn't be going on like this. You couldn't tell me in those days and years before your death. And now you and I will never share those reasons, will we?

We had lunch together recently. I wanted to have lunch with you on a regular basis and get to know you a lot better than we've been able to in recent years. But we never managed to make it a regular occurrence. I'm not blaming you for that. I should have been more insistent, and I could have made the time instead of doing so many other things of lesser importance. It's as much my fault as it is yours. In fact, it's probably more my fault because I'm the big brother and I should have taken the lead on this.

I know another family with five brothers — decent, hard working guys, who get together on a regular basis. They have widely varying lifestyles and viewpoints about this world we find ourselves in. And they talk about their feelings

---

I Always Meant to Tell You...

more than you and I would ever be comfortable doing, bound as we are with our strangely staid mixture of Northern European mores. A strong poker face seems to be required of us at most times. But those guys talk to each other, and they spend time with each other. And, although I'm not sure they've ever actually thought about it in this way, I believe they consider one another to be their best friends.

And now that you're gone, Steve, I've suddenly realized something that I've never realized until this very moment: you were always my best friend.

Bahia de Kino

A Dinner on the Terraza

October 3, 2001

    The shrimp boat that was grounded in the hurricane is no longer on the bar this morning. A sister ship pulled her off yesterday when the tide came in. There may not have been much damage when she was driven onto that long bar of soft sand in the lee of Isla Pelicano. In fact, the Captain probably picked that spot to ground her until the storm blew over. She might even have been one of those distant lighted ships we saw on the horizon last night. We see them on the horizon every night, dragging for the shrimp that will be bathed in butter and garlic and served on a bed of rice to enjoy in any local restaurant along the Calle Mar de Cortez and in the fishing village of Old Kino.

    We've been told that the shrimp boats are required to stay about 10 kilometers offshore to allow the shrimp and other fish some refuge. And to keep the inshore waters from being completely roiled with mud as their nets sweep across the bottom. This morning, there are large schools of fish stirring the surface just off the beach in front of our rented house. Pelicans and gulls follow these schools in their passage down the shore. And there are about a dozen *pangas* fishing inshore this morning, taking advantage of the information provided by the birds.

    Around 9:00 a.m., I stood on the terraza with a cup of hot coffee under a lightly overcast sky, and I peered through binoculars out toward a far horizon heavy with sea-mist. I counted eighteen ships, some only shadows and barely visible, steaming into the bay off Old Kino, to join the dozen or so already riding to their anchors. Once I counted over seventy shrimp boats anchored in the bay. Their home port is Guaymas, but they offload the night's catch at Old Kino and ice it down for market. All day long, port workers prepare and ship the catch while the crews sleep aboard in this protected anchorage. You remember, Steve, the simple and unending daily routine of this fishing outpost. The unending routine of another person's life somehow has a romantic ring to it, don't you think? The routine of our own lives is called drudgery. Life's funny that way.

Yesterday evening Carolyn and I had dinner on the terraza.

Two white plates, with simple painted border designs of yellow and green, held sauteed slices of pork resting beside a rice pilaf. Two white bowls held salads of avocado, lettuce, red pepper and olives. And beside each stood a glass of Bodegas de Santo Tomás cabernet sauvignon from a winery across the Sea in Baja California. The sun had just touched those jagged peaks that grace Isla Tiburón as we raised our glasses and toasted the return of the gentle ocean at Kino Bay. We ate well, and we listened quietly to the voice of the sea. And we watched as the sun nestled deeper into the island to cast its palette of orange and pink and red outward across the furrowed bottoms of scattered clouds before hiding its colors once again till daybreak. The colors of the sky reflected from the clouds onto the golden surface of the sea. And the waves upon the sea were mirrored in the clouds.

An old Mexican man was walking the beach with his wife as the sun set upon one of the more beautiful landscapes on the planet. They were each dressed in simple clothing, and the woman wore an old cotton apron over a faded dress, as if her husband had coaxed her from the stove to experience another stunning sunset. Carolyn had seen the man earlier in the day, carrying a bag, searching the beach for clams and other offerings of the shore. In the evening, he returned with his wife to savor a special moment together in this incomparable place.

I wish very much that you and Janette and the boys could have been here with us to enjoy this evening. The boys would have been at the shore, uninterested in dinner, and they would have interrupted us often with shells and creatures that they found at the edge of the sea. And we would have savored each delicious interruption.

Pelicans and Dolphins

October 4, 2001

The surf was gentle again this morning, Steve, as it was two years ago when you and the family were here. A very gentle surf, maybe six inches high, greeted us each morning as the sun rose. Surf that a baby could play in. Surf that gently nudged beautiful shells ashore at night as if shyly courting the land, leaving morning presents at her door.

We took long quiet walks in the clean light before breakfast, sometimes alone, sometimes in small groups. Those were moments to consider life in general, or to think about the day to come. I saw you and Janette far down the beach silhouetted against the morning sun at the edge of the glistening sea. The kids were busy elsewhere, and you were together in a quiet time. Just the two of you, together and alone for a moment, here in all this beauty. As I look back now, those special vignettes are framed forever, as if they were yesterday.

This morning the early eastern sun angled its rays across placid water beneath a bank of clouds and it splashed brilliant yellow upon the far mountains of Isla Tiburon. Down the shore, a huge flock of pelicans and gulls was circling and diving, moving toward the west, following a school of small fish making its way along the shore. There were probably fifty pelicans in the air circling as they drew closer to where we were standing and watching from the terraza. Then six pelicans folded their wings and dove into the water. Boom, boom, boom, boom, boom, boom. Each hit the surface with tremendous force and bobbed up with a fish in its beak. Four more folded their wings and hit the surface just next to the others.

As they dive, pelicans pull in their broad wings just slightly to maintain control and stay on target. At the last second they tuck themselves into a tightly

---

Bahia de Kino

elongated bullet shape and penetrate the surface, leaving only a tiny splash of spray hanging in the air behind them. Then they bob to the surface to enjoy their meal. The school moves onward down the coast, and the pelicans lift themselves into the air to follow the school for another meal.

And then we saw the dorsal fins we've been waiting for all week. A pair of dolphins was also following the school and breaking the surface at intervals. We followed their graceful progress as they swam westward with the school.

I had plans to do this often with you, Steve, and with Janette, Alec, and Eliot. I thought we might someday have a place here where the family could come for extended visits. And it would also be available to our many friends.

You and I had both finally reached our middle fifties. We had reached that age where most of the big bills were paid and we had some extra discretionary income. We were at the age where we could afford some of those things we had always considered luxuries.

In just a few more years, I'd be completely free and I could actually consider designing a beach home — my very first. I have been looking forward to the challenge for several years now, and I wanted to share the process with you. You and Janette had trusted me with several designs so far, and I thought you would find the process of designing a home for family and visitors to be a fulfilling exercise.

I had considered the possibility that you might want to be involved in a partnership to make it more attainable for both of us to have a beautiful and interesting place to spend time together. A place without phones or TV. A place for conversation in the evening after dinner, or a game of cards, or even one of those annoyingly complicated jigsaw puzzles. It could occupy a corner table for months without disturbing anyone. And there'd be a VCR so we could watch classic movies together with a background soundtrack provided by the sea just beyond our doors. These are just some of the luxuries we've denied ourselves in this modern world. We could have captured them here.

I realize you had a desire to see other parts of the world and that maybe you weren't yet open to the responsibilities of a beach home in Mexico. Still, I had intended to ask you — up until that fatal flight in Alaska. I hadn't even considered asking anyone else but you. And as of now, I still haven't considered it.

So maybe now we'll return to the idea of building a place for ourselves here, a place of refuge for family and friends to enjoy. A place Alec will want to visit often, where he can remember the many good times we all spent together here. Maybe he'll bring his girlfriend down to spend some special time. Maybe someday he'll have children and they'll come here to visit one of the many places where their grandparents found great beauty and joy in their lives.

And maybe those children will savor the special opportunity to experience this place, once thought beautiful by the grandparents they never knew.

Bahía de Kino

The Big Manila Envelope

October 4, 2001

Dear Steve, Janette, and Eliot,

    I have a very large manila envelope filled with cards, letters, testimonials, newspaper articles, and so many other things that have arrived since your deaths were announced on that day back in July. It contains letters of condolence from family members, cousins, aunts, uncles, close friends, acquaintances, one of my ex-wives, the Mayor — people who knew each of you in various ways, and many people I hadn't known before your fatal crash. I brought the envelope to Kino Bay to help with the process of thinking and writing about each of you and the special way that each of you touched my own life.

    And this envelope contains only those letters that arrived at our home. I don't know how many more letters are lying in a basket on a side table at Mom's house, or in a special drawer at Dad's. Or at Elyse's house in Oriental, or at Nancy's in Silver City, or at Joan's in Oceanside. We're a large family with many friends who were impacted by this tragedy.

    Just by itself, this bulging envelope is a very inspiring testimonial by the many people who were touched by each of you in your short and well-lived time here. But I've been so busy just writing down all the many thoughts that I've been dealing with for the past few months that I haven't even looked at the envelope so far. In fact, I'm not even sure exactly where it is at this moment, although I know it's in the house here somewhere. Maybe I'll have a chance to go back through all those things while we're here, and maybe I won't. That's as it will be. I don't intend to push this process in any way. There's so much else I need to tell you that I may not even have time to open the envelope.

Bahia de Kino

And when we return to Alburquerque, I'll put the envelope aside in a special place. And then maybe someday, and it will likely be many years from now, I'll go back through all of these letters and remembrances and I'll recall each of you again and all the many special things that friends and family have said about you.

A Little Sailboat

October 7, 2001

Dearest Eliot,

    We towed that little sailboat behind us all the way down here to Kino Bay. It's the one that we bought from Jon and Joyce. You were there with me to check it out that afternoon when we went bicycle riding together and we stopped by their house to see it.

    I didn't tell you we were going to look at a sailboat when we started riding that day, because I wanted to surprise you. I wanted to see if you might be as interested in sailing as I have been for quite some time now. I think I saw a great deal of interest and expectation that day in a broad smile that spread across your face when you saw her sitting in the driveway on her little trailer. You climbed aboard and "hiked out" with your feet wedged under one of the straps that run fore and aft through the cockpit. It was tough work for those soft young stomach muscles of yours but you kept that big smile on your face as you leaned backward over the rail and you held that pose for as long as you could as you imagined the fresh sea air brushing your face.

    We rode away down old tree-lined streets, and we talked about sailing a small boat on our nearby desert lakes, beneath tall mountains. And we talked about the little coves and hideaways we could explore in her. And we talked, of course, about pirates. And I knew right then that I'd finally found someone who'd spend time out on the water in a little boat, hiked out over the edge of the gun'l, bashing to weather with a smile on his face.

    So we towed her down here through 800 miles of desert to the Sea of Cortez. She's been sitting in the drive since we got here, because the skies have been

Bahia de Kino

overcast as the remnants of the hurricane slowly pack up and move on. The overcast means there's little sun to heat the land and drive the afternoon onshore breezes, and that means we haven't gotten her out on the water. So I still haven't sailed the pretty little boat that you and I looked at in June. I was waiting for you to return from your trip. And when you didn't return, she sat there in Jon and Joyce's driveway, almost forgotten. I didn't feel much like sailing her anymore, after you were gone.

It took a while for me to be able to deal with the little boat, among many other things, after you died. And the question of what to name her suddenly took on a new poignancy with your death. I had thought to name her something like Pirate Princess because I thought you could relate to that. I was going to ask your opinion when you returned, but I was reserving veto power since I was the one who had shelled out the doubloons to buy her.

And now Carolyn has suggested I name her Eliot, because that way I can still spend a lot of time out sailing with Eliot. You would groan over a sailboat named after you though, wouldn't you? Still while I respect your opinion, I'm reserving that veto power I mentioned.

I think I need to take her out and see how she responds to the water. Jon tells me she sails well, that he never capsized her, and that he's never even had green water in the cockpit — but you know what notorious liars sailors are, don't you, Eliot? I'm sure that you heard plenty about sailors in your short tenure here. So I think we'll take her out soon and see how she does.

And now the sun has returned to Kino Bay to spread the afternoon surface of the ocean with flakes of silver. The time has come to go sailing in that little boat that you and I looked at together a few months back, our *barquito de velas*. I'll take her out and see if she suggests a name for herself.

We'll go sailing tomorrow. But it will be a sad occasion. It won't feel the same out there on the briny deep without you, without the two of us hiked far out over the windward rail chanting at the top of our lungs, "Fifteen men on a dead man's chest! Yo, ho, ho, and a bottle of rum!"

Your Desk at Home, Steve

October 7, 2001

I remember, years ago, Steve, that you had an average-sized desk and there was a lot of clutter on it. That's a trait that seems to run in our family.

Our Dad has an office with no visible open space anywhere in it. Instead, there are piles of books, papers and magazines on every horizontal surface. Each pile has a theme and is a vertical collection of related materials that might be important to someone someday. Bette just requires him to keep all his mess inside the doorway so it doesn't intrude upon the living area.

When I visited our Uncle Jim in St. Petersburg, Florida, his tiny, shabby apartment had the same design motif. He moved several piles off the couch to make space for us to sit down.

My own office has its own piles of material, but there's a lot less of it than in any of the others I just mentioned. And every bit of it is tremendously important. As least to me.

And none of us really understands how those executives with clean desks ever get anything done. Where's their supporting data, anyway? I have this suspicion that they just dispense with all that supporting data and other troublesome facts, and they wing it. In our family we would consider that cheating; but most people probably wouldn't know the difference, anyway. They're just going to believe whoever's smooth and glib and tells them what's simple enough to understand. In the end, the facts and the data don't really matter to most people. The successful executive is the one who recognizes this one fundamental fact, and dispenses with all the rest.

After the accident I had a chance to use your new desk. It was a big long wrap-around model with lots of horizontal surface. Even so, there was still no

Bahia de Kino

room to begin the painful process of deciphering your busy professional life and notifying your extensive list of clients. We had to go through the process of trying to organize at least some of those important piles of paper to create a small space to work on. And eventually we began to wade through the sad remnants of a very busy and effective life.

Just to the left of your computer sat that broad-brimmed western farmer hat you liked to wear out on the property. The one you put on to go check the old apple trees in that little remnant orchard at the back of the place. Or to check the ditch water going to that stretch of alfalfa by the drive coming in from Fourth Street. Or that band of foliage you helped to plant along the north property line to provide food and shelter for birds and small animals. I know it brought you a great deal of pleasure each time a big pheasant strode out of the brush to scratch for grubs in the grassy area that doubles for a badminton court, or football field, or just a place for kids to roll in the grass. And when the vegetables began to ripen in the communal garden area, you wore that big floppy hat to go check on things.

You always had time for all those things that are important to family and community, and you still got the things done that society considers important.

Even with your messy desk.

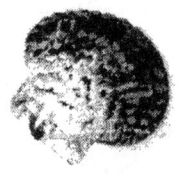

Trash on the Beach

October 8, 2001

Each day something different appears on the shore below our terraza — depending, I suppose, on the currents and such. Each day, different and beautiful varieties of shells and other relics of the sea decorate the shore. Unfortunately, there's also a lot of trash here in paradise, covered with salt and tangled with seaweed.

I hate to even bring it up, but the amount of trash that washes ashore here is very disturbing for such a small community. Mostly, it's a mix of plastic bottles, plastic bags, plastic wrappers, plastic beach shoes. We are in the process of burying the most beautiful parts of the world in a layer of cheap plastic trash.

Some of the trash comes from picnics on the beach. We're a very messy species, regardless of our nationality. After a weekend here, especially a big holiday weekend, there's a lot of debris lying around. Most trash left during the day is blown by afternoon onshore winds into the lee of houses along the shore.

The strongest daily breezes are the onshore winds that blow in the afternoons here, and they bring things in from the sea. Most of this stuff seems to come from those who carelessly use this sheltered sea, including the gringo sport fishermen here. But it's still hot here in Kino, and very few of the snowbirds who drive down from the US and Canada in winter have arrived yet.

I have my suspicions that much of the plastic we pick up each day in our walks along the shore comes from the shrimp boats that dredge the sea each night — but I don't have proof, of course. They just seem like the logical source for a lot of it.

Late at night, the masthead lights of the shrimp boat fleet look like a distant string of fairy candles quietly adrift upon a distant horizon. Yet the crews are hard at work, hauling nets, sorting fish from shrimp, repairing torn sections of net. It isn't easy work.

Bahia de Kino

They break now and then for a snack, a midnight meal, maybe a bite of *desayuno* at daybreak. The crew on a fishing boat stop to eat when there's a break in the routine. They pull out tamales, bags of chips and snack foods they stashed aboard back in port. Empty bags and bottles are tossed off the stern to disappear in the night, forgotten in the dark turbulence of the wake. Forgotten, that is, until it washes ashore here on the beach in Kino Bay a day or so later. Some days are worse than others, and I don't know why. It may be that one of the shrimp boats passed closer to shore last night. Some days, masses of plastic trash tangled with heavy polypropylene fishing line and pieces of discarded netting, litter the beach.

I walk down to the water and I pass several pieces of garbage. I pick them up and stuff them into the sand so they won't blow away. I'll gather them later and put them into a trash bag. As I step into the water, a couple of large plastic bags are swirling in the surf. I snag them and walk back to where I've stashed the others. I go farther out into the surf and find more pieces of plastic garbage I don't want to run into while I'm swimming. I scoop them out of the water and return to shore to leave them with the others. I head back out through the surf and dive beneath a wave before I see any more of it.

I don't want to appear ungrateful for the rare opportunity to be here. We are guests in this country, and I don't want to complain too much. I only want to mention the realities of life here. This is not an unspoiled paradise. There are problems on this beautiful stretch of the Mexican coast.

Seashells in the Morning

October 9, 2001

It's an especially gorgeous day, Steve. There's much to tell you about the shore today.

The sea brought beautiful new presents to the shore today. Shells of all kinds and colors, and shapes that we had never seen before.

It may have to do with Juliette, the hurricane that passed over us last weekend. She must have stirred the bottom with tremendous force, driving these shells, and their inhabitants, to the edges of the sea. As high tide floods onto the land, shells are pushed ashore and left on the drying sand as the water retreats.

We walk on the hard-packed surface of wet sand and pick up huge yellow clam shells, *almejas*, tightly closed, their occupants still very much alive within. Local people walk the beach to gather these clams from the shore. They slice the clams open, wash them carefully, and drench the muscle with lime juice. It's a quick and easy dinner of fresh raw clam.

Carolyn boiled one of these clams and minced the meat to include in a delicious dish of sauteed tomato slices and green peppers over angel-hair pasta. The secret is in mincing the meat, otherwise, it's as chewy as rubber. It was a delicious meal for the two of us, with a glass of *vino tinto* on the terraza as the sun set over Isla Tiburon in a halo of orange and red.

Usually when we find a shell whose occupant still resides there, we toss it far out beyond the breaking surf so it has a chance to get to deeper water. The gulls who patrol this beach after each ebbing tide would prefer we not return these potential dinners to the sea. And the shore crabs that occupy tiny holes among the dunes would prefer that, too. They would rather we leave them for the day's sun to cook open to that certain smelly perfection preferred by crabs and seabirds.

Bahia de Kino

Still, we toss them as far as we can toward open water. There will be others for the gulls and crabs to dine on.

But the empty shells that wash ashore here in astounding numbers every day are enough to keep a curious soul busy. There are those large yellow clams with smooth shells. There are other clamshells, almost as large, and smooth with broad burgundy bands. And there are some with delicate ridges that look almost like tree rings. They compel you to run your fingers across them.

Huge multicolored snail shells wash up here. And very large scallop shells, as fragile as fine china. There are some that were called turkey wings in a sea shell display box I got for Christmas when I was about ten years old. And there are cowries, lots of them, big and small, of many colors, everywhere we look. Some are occupied by live hermit crabs, and we throw them back into the sea. And there are some of the most gorgeous big shells that look like Triton horns with spikes all over. Some are zebra-striped in black and white, and others have a pinkish tint.

There are cockles, and whelks, and winged oysters that look like eagles in flight, and cones, and turbans, and mussels, and stromebs — interesting name, stromebs. There are more different kinds of shells here than we can easily comprehend. We need to get a good book on the subject. A book like the one I leafed through today at the Prescott College branch at the west end of town. We hear they conduct at least some of their classes in kayaks.

There are seeds — seaweed seeds, I guess — just starting to sprout. They came ashore in large numbers for days after the hurricane. It's nature's way of cutting back on the population so there's enough food for the rest. It's a nautical version of the legend of Icarus, of reminding the creatures of the sea not to venture too close to the shore.

There are other surprising creatures of the sea that come ashore just outside our door. The other morning we found a small octopus lying dead upon the shore. It didn't appear to be damaged in any way as it lay there on the wet sand, its tentacles curled inward in a final embrace. It may have been the victim of a marine virus, or food poisoning, or maybe it was killed by the increased water temperatures that spawn hurricanes here each fall. When we first arrived, the sea felt like warm bath water as we swam. It felt good to us, but to a creature who can't escape, those higher temperatures might be fatal.

That little octopus lying on the shore reminded me of once when I was swimming in these shallow waters several years ago and I reached down to grab a clam shell from the bottom. As I turned it over, I saw the tiniest octopus hiding on the inside, struggling against the surface tension of the thinning water as the bowl of the shell emptied into the sea. He was no bigger than my thumbnail, and I almost didn't even see him at all until I noticed some kind of motion in the shell. I studied him for just a moment or two, and I wondered what he might be thinking at the sight of this huge land-bound monster staring down at him. And then I put him, and his shell, back on the bottom.

When we were here last year, we found the carcass of a very large squid that had washed ashore. Its body was almost a foot in diameter and about three feet long. It was an impressive sight, and we wondered what had killed this creature of the very deep water that lies far offshore. It might have been caught in one of the shrimp boat nets, and then discarded overboard. The tentacles were gone — maybe eaten by various sea creatures as it drifted on the surface. If I recall correctly, the tentacles on a squid may be more than twice as long as its body, so we were looking at a once-sizable creature that now lay inert upon the sand, a sad reminder of the large animals that inhabit the depths of this sea.

Yesterday I saw something else, small dark and motionless, sitting on the wet sand as I returned to shore after swimming. It wasn't colorful, so it didn't quickly catch my eye. It was just something that I noticed among clumps of seaweed as I looked at shells lying in the surf. As I grew closer I saw that it was a small bird, just sitting there on the sand and being brushed now and then by each small wave of the returning sea. Then I thought I saw it move. I stepped closer and tried to nudge it with my foot; it pulled its head back to dodge me. I stopped and I looked down at this once-proud creature of the air that had lived out its life here where the sea kisses the desert, and I wondered if there was anything that I could do. The bird looked at me and then looked away. He seemed to wish that I would go, that I would leave him in peace to spend his remaining moments of life at the edge of the sea that had provided for him all these years. The sea that would soon reclaim another one of its own.

I looked away toward the ancient, jagged shape of Isla Pelicano, lying anchored forever off this shore, and I felt the afternoon breeze upon my face.

Recently, I have become more acutely aware of death and more intimately connected to it than I have ever thought possible. I realize that there is a time and a place for everything, and that death is an intimate part of our brief lives upon this unique and beautiful planet. Each of us has our time, our place, and our moment here. And no more.

I looked back down again toward this small bird resting at my feet in its final moments on the eternal shore of Kino Bay. The bird stared out toward the sea. I turned away in silence, and walked up the shore to the house.

Bahia de Kino

Many lives are nurtured by the ocean here. We've barely begun to know them in the brief time we have here each year. It's become clear, in our daily walks, that we need a decent book about sea life in general, so we'll know something about its daily offerings. And especially about the amazing shells we find here along this portion of the Sea of Cortez.

"Viewable"

October 10, 2001

"Viewable." It's a terrible term I'd never heard before. Terrible in implication, clinically accurate and impersonal.

As a result of the accident, I now know that emergency medical personnel use this term to describe the condition of bodies extracted from demolished cars, buses, trains — and aircraft. The term "Viewable" means the remains are sufficiently presentable for viewing during a funeral service — after the embalmer performs his considerable magic to preserve the deceased long enough for the family to pay their last respects. It's a gruesome term.

In the crash of Nancy Lewis's plane, local authorities identified the bodies of those found in the front seats as Nancy, the pilot,... and Steve, my only brother. The bodies of Janette and Eliot were in the two back seats. According to authorities, the back seat passengers were considered "viewable." The front passengers were not.

Small aircraft, especially those built several decades ago, were not designed for safe impact with the ground. It's an understandable problem, complicated by the high speeds attained in an airplane crash. The interiors of most older planes contain hard surfaces that become lethal weapons in a crash. Considering how many billions of us have managed to populate the planet, it's hard to grasp how fragile the human body really is. It's surprisingly difficult to survive a car crash at more than 30 miles per hour. Police files are filled with reports of those who didn't.

Consider the possibilities in a small plane probably exceeding 150 miles per hour when it strikes the ground. There's little or nothing in those aircraft to cushion the impact because most designers long ago dismissed the idea of crash survivability and concentrated instead on aircraft reliability. The results are clear in the remarkable safety records posted by large commercial aircraft on regularly

---

Bahia de Kino

scheduled routes. The crash of an airliner full of passengers, a rare occurrence, is a troubling news story.

But a look at accident investigations posted on the NTSB web site, shows an alarming number of crashes by small aircraft, and with a high percentage of fatalities — on the order of a death per day over the few months of data I scanned on the Internet one evening. That's far less than the daily carnage on our nation's highways, but many fewer people fly in small aircraft. I don't know the deaths-per-mile ratio, but it's simply dangerous to travel in a small plane. If a car runs out of gas, or the engine stalls, the consequences are rarely fatal. Small aircraft are far less forgiving.

And remains found in the wreckage can be difficult to look at. Few of us, I imagine, are capable of recovering and identifying dead accident victims. The first person on the scene of this accident was a friend of Nancy's who recognized her plane lying broken on the ground, in a remote area of the Alaskan woods. He landed in a dangerous place and climbed down to the site of the wreckage, hoping to find someone alive. I'm grateful for his willingness to risk his own life in a futile effort to help possible survivors. And I'm very sorry he had to be the first to see what must have been a gruesome sight.

Of those who came later to extract the bodies, I can only thank them, and all the others who do this on a regular basis. Their difficult work spared our family this last gruesome look at our loved ones. We don't even think about the job these people face each day until, tragically, we suddenly need them.

Steve, I didn't want to see you this way. I can't even imagine it. I was the one who was most likely to end up this way. I never believed, in all our years together, that this could happen to you. Especially not you, the careful one.

The family chose to avoid the added trauma of showing the bodies of Janette and Eliot at the service and asked that all the bodies be cremated in Fairbanks. The choice was influenced by the distance from Alburquerque, and by paperwork problems at the Alaska State Coroner's Office before the remains could be released. Fortunately, John Robertson, family friend and emergency room physician was working in Anchorage at the time and was able to expedite the process. There was much to be done in Alburquerque, and nothing that a family member could do in Alaska.

The cremains were shipped home together for a quiet family ceremony at your church, St. Michael's and all Angels, in the week following the public memorial service. Father Bryan led this sad occasion as we placed your urns in the sanctuary by the door.

And so it was that I never saw you alive again, Steve. Or Janette. Or Eliot.

I Always Meant to Tell You...

The Mice of Kino Bay

October 11, 2001

Dear Eliot,

    I need to tell you about our adventures with a very large family of mice who adopted this house as their own vacation hideaway before we arrived. There's something about those fuzzy little puffballs that is unbelievably cute to a nine-year-old like yourself, and even to certain older soft-hearted folks as well — although not, perhaps, to your mother.

    When you peer over the edge of a bucket and see one or two little gray and fuzzy fellows looking back up with big brown eyes, their inquisitive noses twitching in the air, it's really hard not to like them. Especially as you consider that the next portion of their little lives is entirely up to you. At this point, you have to choose whether to kill them or not. "Destroy them" is the euphemism preferred by society, but that sounds a little too clinical and clean for me. It implies that they simply disappear or something, and nobody suffers. It doesn't suggest that they'll be stomped to death under someone's heel. There's no doubt that's a quick and simple end, and the mice will suffer very little, but there's something brutal about it that probably does far more harm to the person charged with their 'disposal.' At least, that's how it affects me.

    Consider the concept of "undesirable critters" for a moment. We don't want to be sharing our homes with mice. They live in dark and damp locations that breed bacteria and disease. During the Middle Ages that mice and rats spread the Black Plague throughout Europe. It's probably one of the reasons that the philosopher, Thomas Hobbes, described the life of the poor in his time as "nasty, brutish, and short," or words to that effect.

Bahia de Kino

All of us who emigrated from Europe many centuries later can be thankful that our ancestors survived the Plague, and many others before and since. Maybe they understood that mice and rats are notoriously effective at spreading disease. If one person in a village caught a disease, mice spread it very quickly as they scampered from house to house in search of food until the entire village was infected. We learned a hard lesson that mice are not good companions. And I agree completely with that.

So, what to do with a bunch of mice who seem very happy to enjoy their lives in the home we've rented on the beach? We can't live with them, and yet we don't want to be cruel. So what do we do?

Good question, don't you think, Eliot?

We became aware of the mouse problem when we heard a strange noise at night coming from a nice wooden handcrafted Mexican ottoman that was sitting in a corner of the bedroom. There was a kind of gnawing sound coming from that corner late at night, and we assumed it was due to creaking in the house, or something like that. But the house was well built of concrete block and steel, well plastered, with no cracks. It wasn't creaking. After several days, we looked more closely and found, um, "mouse presents." They were lying all over the floor under the ottoman. In the cabinets, we found even more "gifts" from the mice. We didn't want to disrupt their "mouse family values" but we needed to do something about them, and soon.

At first we were very surprised that there were even mice in this house on a seashore at the edge of a desert. It's solid masonry — even the interior walls are masonry — and there were no cracks they could crawl through. They must have gotten in under the front door; mice can get very tiny when they want to. The house was very clean when we rented it and there wasn't any food left lying around, so we assumed that's why they were eating the furniture. We don't think they had permission to stay here while the house was empty. We decided to "request" these mice to leave.

We looked for mouse traps, but there weren't any in the closets, the cabinets or the *bodega* (the storeroom) outside by the front gate. So we went down the street to that little store called the Super Juliana to see what he had on the shelf. He had packages of 'glue boards' that you put into the cabinets, with a little cheese snack in the center. Then you wait until there's a mouse stuck to it. We bought a couple and they actually worked very well. In the morning we had a couple of mice stuck to them. The mice looked pretty forlorn lying there, stuck and helpless.

Your Aunt Carolyn and I looked at each other and said, "OK, we've caught some. What do we do with them now?"

Aunt Carolyn was raised on a farm, and they didn't spend a lot of time worrying about the morality of mouse control. They cause tremendous damage to food supplies and anything else that's stored in the barn. And there were lots of mice everywhere around the farm since they have several litters per year. Getting rid of them wasn't really possible in the fertile farm lands of the American Midwest. Just keeping them under control was tough enough.

But here we were, looking at two little mice hopelessly stuck to a couple of glue boards, and just terrified. I got an empty plastic 5-gallon paint bucket out of the bodega. Then I picked up each glue board with a pair of kitchen tongs and placed it in the bottom.

"OK. Now what?" I thought to myself as Aunt Carolyn shook her head and smiled. It was up to me to do something with them.

"OK, mice." I said, mostly to myself because they were busy trying to get loose and didn't seem to be listening, "Let's go for a walk." I stuck the "mouse tongs" into my back pocket and I picked up the bucket.

I took the bucket, mice and all, out the front door and down the street, to a little side street that leads straight out a big low area behind the dunes. There are plenty of bushes and plants and nutritious seeds out there to keep a couple of mice fed and occupied for a while. I'd just take them out there, and pry them off the glue boards, and they can go merrily on to the next phase of their little lives. Actually, the next phase of their lives probably involves being a dinner guest for a snake or an owl, but that's just part of nature. At least they'll do some good that way, and they're not my problem any more.

But it was another thing to get those two little mice pried off those glue boards. I would carefully pull one tiny paw loose and then the mouse would get his tail stuck while he was struggling. Neither mouse seemed to listen to my instructions about how to stay unstuck after I got one part loose. I had to hold the glue board upside down so they would hang there while I got each tiny foot off the board. Meanwhile, thousands of mosquitoes decided to have a feast on me. When it rains, especially after hurricane Julieta, that low area behind the dunes collects a lot of shallow water, and the mosquitoes breed out there. There were literally millions of them in the air and I was their closest target. I worked as fast as I could without hurting the mice, although there was an occasional squeak of displeasure. Soon they were both on their way, scampering toward the tall brush. And I was on my way, running away from all those mosquitoes.

Bahia de Kino

I thought how convenient this was for a snake who might be living out there in the bushes. His own mice delivery service — kind of like Domino's Pizza, mouse-flavored. And I don't even get a tip.

I stuck the two glue boards together and put them into a trash can on my way back to the house and that was the end of it. At least until we noticed more mouse droppings a day or so later.

We put out a couple more glue boards and we got two more mice, except that one of them was only stuck by the tail and he took off running when we opened the cabinet — with the glue board right behind him. He disappeared under the stove. We tilted the stove out, but he was gone. , We never saw him or the glue-board again. After prying another mouse loose — this time with a spatula — we decided to try something different. It was a technique that actually hadn't worked at all when we tried it once, many years ago.

We had a mouse once in our little house on Orchard Place. He wasn't much trouble, except for the droppings, of course. He would scamper out into the middle of the room where Carolyn was writing, and he would sit on his hind legs to look up at her. I'd see him now and then looking at me from behind a chair or something. We even grew fond of him, but we both knew it wasn't a good idea to share the house this way.

So one evening, I got a big plastic bucket from the shed and we taped a piece of newspaper over the open end. Then we took a razor blade and carefully cut an X in the top. We set this bucket-trap next to the mouse's favorite bookshelf, with a little board leading onto the top and we baited it with some tiny bits of cheese. Then we each went back to our reading and we waited.

Within half an hour, there was a bunch of noise from the area of the bucket, and I called out to Carolyn, "Well dear, I think we have a mouse."

I set my book down and I walked quietly over to the bucket so as not to alarm the little fellow any more than necessary. I squatted down and I carefully lifted one corner to peek inside at our captive. But the bucket was empty.

"Well I'll be." I said as I looked inside a second time to make sure I hadn't missed seeing him hiding. But there are no places to hide in a round plastic bucket.

"Well I guess he jumped back out or something." I called to Carolyn, "He sure isn't in the bucket." She just laughed and kept reading.

I sat there for moment on my haunches and looked over the situation to see if there was some way we could improve upon this method. Surely there was a way to do this without the mouse being able to jump back out, if that's what had really happened. And as I sat there studying the bucket, the top, and following that little board to where it rested on the top of several books, I saw two beady little eyeballs, peeking out from behind a book, studying me.

My jaw dropped as the mouse looked at me. Then he looked at the bucket. Then he looked back at me. He seemed to be asking, "Hey, what's going on here? I haven't done anything very bad since I got here, have I? I just ate a few crumbs, that's all. I thought we were friends. What's with this bucket trap, anyway?"

He was wise to the bucket, so I put it away and ended up buying one of those very expensive have-a-heart type traps to catch him and we caught him a few days later. We made a special trip to let him go somewhere down in the bosque along the river. And we left a nice piece of cheese there, too, so he wouldn't go hungry. In the end I felt good about it, but I missed seeing our little friend around the house.

But we didn't bring that have-a-heart trap with us to the house in Mexico, so we tried the bucket idea again. We hoped these mice couldn't jump as high as that little guy back home.

And it worked. We set it up next to an open cabinet and we got a mouse the first night out. I took him out there behind the dunes and dumped him out. Then I watched as he hightailed it into the brush. The mouse delivery service was back in action, and I headed quickly back to the house. Now, without me hanging around out there dealing with mice stuck to gluepads, the mosquitoes were going to stay hungry.

But by now we were starting to wonder if there was any end to the mouse population in this house. So far, we had evicted around seven mice — seven nice little snake-meals — and we always seemed to come up with more. A day passed without mice in the bucket and we hoped that was the end of it.

But then one morning we had three baby mice in the bucket. They weren't actually new-borns, but they were about half the size of the others and they were really cute. They scampered around in the bucket and tried to jump up the sides when they saw us, but it was far too high for them. I took them outside and dumped them out on the other side of the dunes with their parents.

And then this morning we had three more small ones, but they weren't in the bucket this time. They were in the sink. Aunt Carolyn put small plastic containers over two of them, but the other one decided to jump down the garbage disposal. So now we had another interesting problem on our hands. I got the flashlight and looked down into the disposal. And I can tell you that it's not a pleasant sight. But I saw our little mouse looking cold and bedraggled and hiding along one

---

Bahia de Kino

side. I was able to lift him out with those kitchen tongs and drop him into a small plastic container for a trip outside and beyond the dunes to join the others.

At this point, we have no idea if that's all the mice or not, but we've done our best to relocate the population. I hope we're done with it for now, and I hope the mice are enjoying themselves very nicely — somewhere else far out in the desert. Far from here.

Los Naranjeros

October 11, 2001

Dear Eliot,

On our last weekend here we decided to take a break from this beautiful home by the beach and go in to Hermosillo for a couple of days. I think you will find this part very interesting because one of the main reasons we went into town was to catch a Naranjeros game.

As we have spent more time here in the state of Sonora, we have gotten to know more about the people and the things they like to do. One of those things I wanted to share with you someday was to see a baseball game here and to watch the home team play. That's what we did on a Sunday afternoon.

It was the first home game of the season for the Naranjeros (the Orange Growers) and the home crowd was out in force. If the Dukes' fans had been this enthusiastic, Alburquerque would have kept their ball team. We left Kino Bay after breakfast and headed for town. It was around 11 am when we found the stadium, called Estadio Hector Espina, and bought our tickets. The place was almost sold out already, and all they could sell us were two seats in different rows — one behind the other. With a crowd like that expected at the game, we thought it would be a good idea to find a hotel somewhere and then catch a bus back to the stadium in time for the game. Mexican cities have very good bus service, so we knew it wouldn't be a problem to get there, and it would be a lot better than driving around in strange traffic after dark. I don't know for sure where all those Mexican cars acquire their dented fenders, but I have my suspicions. So, taking a bus just seemed like a really good idea. We only had to figure out which bus would get us back to the hotel after the game. It would be the kind of adventure we enjoy.

Bahia de Kino

First, we spent the early afternoon looking around the city and getting our bearings. We have been through Hermosillo many times over the past decade, but we know very little about the place. It's a city of maybe a million people, so there has to be something going on here. It was time we took a good look around.

We stopped to eat at Sanborn's and watch well-dressed Mexican families enjoying themselves at Sunday lunch after Mass. Sanborn's has a very good bookstore, and we are always tempted whenever we stop. It's a good way to practice our Spanish.

Later we found an area of old buildings and narrow winding streets, like you see in most Mexican cities, although they looked less well-kept than in tourist-oriented cities. And we found an up-scale neighborhood called the Colonia Centenario not far from the Universidad de Sonora. On one corner there was a very interesting restaurant called La Casa del Patrón that caused us to stop to ask a few questions. We'd already had lunch, but we made a plan to come back for breakfast.

We picked a hotel that happened to be named the Hotel Kino. It was near the Universidad de Sonora and we wanted to take a long walk around that area on Monday. We stashed our stuff in the room and caught the bus. We arrived at the stadium early for the opening festivities at three o'clock and for the first pitch at five o'clock. I remember that whenever we took you to a Dukes game, Eliot, you wanted to be sure we were there for the first pitch. And you always wanted to stay till the very end. We'd have done that in Hermosillo, as well.

The stadium, the parking lot, and half the street, were crowded with Naranjeros fans when we got there. The noise was deafening. I think maybe Mexican fans have more fun than US fans because they sure make a lot more noise. As we entered the gate, there was a band playing at full volume under the concrete stands. It was hard to tell what tune they were playing because of all the echoes in that small space filled with yelling fans, but I think volume was more important than melody.

We went up a ramp that curved around the outside of the stadium and found our seats. There was a very loud announcer yelling over the roar of the excited crowd. And there was another guy, standing in the walkway in front of the seats with a bullhorn, trying to be heard over the rest of the noise. It was high carnival at its richest, and I know you would have loved the wonderful absurdity of it.

These fans had good reason to yell. The Naranjeros were *Campeones del Temporada, 2000-2001* — last year's Champions of their league, *la Liga Mexicana del Pacifico*. Their team was also coming off a 12 to 1 victory over the Aguilas (the

Eagles) of Mexicali on Friday night, so they were pumped. But the Aguilas were out for blood after being humiliated in front of their hometown fans in their season opener, so the stakes were high. It looked like it was going to be a great game.

First they passed out trophies from last year and honored all the players for their efforts. Then a couple of parachuters landed on the field. A guy brought out two gigantic beach balls, painted like baseballs, for the fans to knock around the stands for a while in an impromptu, no-rules, volleyball game. There were bright red Tecate signs everywhere, and a couple of large inflatable beer cans stood at each end of the bleachers.

It was a hot afternoon, the crowd was happy, and we were glad we had seats in the shade. I left my watch somewhere about a month ago, but judging by the sun angle it was time for a beer.

The first few innings went by uneventfully, except that every time I stood up to stretch, or just look around, I noticed a lot of people looking in my direction. I think that your Aunt Carolyn and I probably set an all-time record number for gringos in the stadium. I sure couldn't blame those folks for being curious about us. They really enjoyed watching us cheering on the Naranjeros.

About the fourth inning, just about when the kids might be getting bored, a bunch of girls passed out skinny white balloons to the crowd. They were each about four feet long, the balloons that is, and along one edge they said, *"Bebe leche...Naranjeros,"* or something like that. I think they were encouraging the kids to drink milk, and that's always a good idea. The kids twisted them into headbands and into dog shapes and shook them in the air when the home team got a hit.

Sometime around the sixth inning, the Naranjeros' team mascot rolled a giant box wrapped like a present out onto the field and stopped by the Second Base Umpire. When he opened it, a tall beautiful girl stepped out and handed the Umpire a nice cold drink. Then she wiped his forehead and massaged his shoulders before stepping back into the box for the trip back off the field. It sure doesn't hurt to be on the good side of the umpires!

But later in the game, when the mascot pulled another large present out to where the First Base Umpire was standing, a bunch of kids jumped out and chased him around for a while. Maybe he made a bad call, or something. The fans loved it.

The home team won the game that night with a 2 to 1 victory. The Naranjeros did their best to keep the fans happy, and we'll be back again next year.

And, Eliot, I only wish that you could join us there. I know that you would love every minute of it.

Bahia de Kino

Many Questions

October 11, 2001

I have questions, Steve, many questions, born of confusion and frustration, and all of them now unanswerable. But they trouble me still, and I have to ask them.

So what, then, is personal safety? When, after all, are we safe enough?

You and Janette were concerned about the safety of your children. It's a parent's primary job in life. You did things the right way, from child restraints in the back seat of your old Volvo station wagon to hats and sunblock lotion. And you never knowingly risked the lives of your children in any way. You were very careful people.

You worried about Alec's safety when he went away to BMX camp in Pennsylvania. And during his school years, you dealt with bullies who picked on the tall, gawky kid in class. You and I could both relate to that; we were the tall, gawky kids at our school. But you could not fight Alec's battles for him. And you told him so. This was wise advice for your oldest son. Alec learned to get along with the other kids, and he grew strong so that nobody dared pick on him. He's a handsome young man today, and I know you would both be very proud of him.

Eliot, who was with you on the plane that day, was different. This happy, fair-haired young fellow was prone to serious sunburn, so you kept him under hat and sunblock; and he wore a long-sleeved shirt in our intense high desert summers. It wasn't easy for a lad with the outgoing athletic interests of Eliot, but you kept him safe from the damaging sun that could cause him problems later in life. And he understood why.

You were concerned about the safety of your children, yet refused to hide them from a world of experience that lay beyond the horizon. You took Alec to

Bahia de Kino

Guatemala when he was very young, to visit Nancy and Audón and to see where his mother had spent her residency working with the impoverished clients of the Baerhorst Clinic. A couple of years ago, you took Alec and Eliot to Bolivia to visit Nancy and Audón and their cousin, Elysanna, when they relocated there. You drove them both cross-country to family reunions in southern Kentucky.

This summer, you took Eliot on a long drive north to Janette's birthplace in Idaho, then onward into Canada, and up the Al-Can Highway to Fairbanks where Janette did another medical stint many years ago, flying to back country villages in the winter. And that's where the three of you died together in the crash of a small plane, in the course of another family adventure.

So where do we draw the line? Where is the boundary beyond which we dare not go? Can we visit foreign countries? Fly in small aircraft? Drive a car cross-country — arguably the most dangerous thing most of us ever do? Or should we live safely in our homes and never dare to tread in that dangerous world just outside our door?

In *The Republic*, Plato draws his famous "Analogy of the Cave." He imagines the limited perspective of a person imprisoned deep within a cavern who only sees the shadows of events reflected by candlelight upon a wall. That is all he will know of these events, since he has never seen them in person. There are people in this large country of ours who feel no need to experience the other peoples and regions of this vast world and to really understand them. They only know that which is written or spoken for them by others. They see the flickers of candlelight upon a wall, and they accept it as reality.

You wanted more for your kids. You refused to hide and wish the world away. They deserved more than that. They were both intelligent and curious lads who made the most of each new opportunity to learn about their world. They deserved the opportunity to experience other lands and make new friends there. You provided that for them in a thoughtful and careful manner. And no-one can fault you for it.

During those final fatal moments when that small plane plunged to the Alaskan earth, you were both — you must have been — thinking this cannot be! That suddenly all your concern had been wasted. That you had ultimately failed your children and each other. But nobody here among your family, nor among your many friends, can fault your decision to go onward with life's adventure, to fly north together in a small plane to a distant lake, on that beautiful day.

Sailing with the Sea Gods

October 11, 2001

Dearest Eliot,

    We took her out yesterday upon the beautiful Sea of Cortez, that fine little sailboat we've planned to name Elioto, the name your mother and father called you in many moments of affection. It seems to be the most appropriate name for a little sailboat that I had hoped you and I would spend many hours aboard exploring enchanted waters in the vast deserts of New Mexico, and northern Mexico.
    Yesterday was a typical, wonderful, Fall day here on the Mexican coast, with a brisk little breeze of 15 to 20 knots blowing onto this southerly shore from a southeasterly direction that brought it just over the shoulder of Pelican Island. There were some whitecaps, called white ponies by sailors, as we launched from the ramp at the far western end of Kino Bay, just beyond that jagged hill of volcanic red rock that marks the end of the beach. A fellow helped us launch, although he apparently had little or no experience with boats.
    He looked at her and asked *"¿No hay motor?"*
    No, we assured him, there was no motor. It was a *barco de velas*, a sailboat.
    "¿Pura velas?" he asked.
    Yep. Just sails.
    We left the shore and were quickly on our way, out past the rocks, under jib alone at first, just to get the feel of her. Then we hoisted the main, and her balanced sails brought her nose up into the wind. There's a big black cannon on her main that I know you would appreciate, Eliot; it identifies her as a Mutineer. Her tiller felt good with both sails up, and we sailed westward into the sea on port tack. Then we cleared the outer edge of the volcanic promontory and tacked her

---

Bahia de Kino

through the wind. We settled into a starboard tack that took us around the forbidding rocky base of the hill, and down the beach front toward that little home we've rented for the month that we've needed to get away and to remember you and your parents. There's something about a day at sea that makes many things come clearer in the mind, but there's still a lot about what happened to the three of you that I think I'll never understand.

Our little boat settled happily into a windward tack, taking the wave and the wind in her stride. We balanced her with our weight, and she rode over the waves with ease, occasionally slapped by a playful wave across the nose that sent a refreshing spray over her bow and onto the intrepid sailors aboard. She was in her element, glad to be free of the land and fully alive once more upon the water. I kept her nose in the wind, just short of pinching and luffing the jib, and we watched the homes that lined the shore fall rapidly away behind us. I steered for the far eastern end of the beach and we stayed far enough offshore that we wouldn't have to tack again till we reached the very end of this great curving scimitar of sand.

As we neared the eastern end, the sun was low in the sky, and we knew that it would soon disappear behind the distant mountains of Isla Tiburon. It was time to jibe her around and come back down the beach. We came about, and we stayed in close to the beach with the wind now over her port quarter. If we strayed into shallow water, we could pull her nose up into the wind and claw our way off the shore. We stayed just behind the breaking waves with maybe a foot or so of water to spare beneath our keel. She drafts about four feet, so we had to stay out far enough to keep her keel above the sand in those troughs between the waves. We passed groups of swimmers and people walking on the beach who waved at the happy mariners aboard. And in your honor, we broke into a song that you knew quite well:

> *Fifteen men on a dead man's chest!*
> *Yo, ho, ho, and a bottle of rum!*
> *Drink and the devil hath done for the rest!*
> *Yo, ho, ho, and a bottle of rum!*

We rounded the headland and beached her on the sand. And then I suggested to Carolyn that we offer our "helper" a ride. Carolyn's Spanish is far better than mine, so she approached him about it. His jaw dropped noticeably.

"*¿De veras?*" he stammered excitedly.

"Yes, really!" we assured him.

His name was Jesus, and he was out relaxing on a Saturday away from the city. He was enjoying looking at the water and sipping a beer or two. The offer of a boat ride with a tall gringo came as a complete surprise.

We were quickly back in the boat and on our way from the shore. He was seated on the floor in a tangle of ropes and lines going in every direction. It was time to trim the jib, so I asked him to pull in on the starboard jib sheet.

"*¡Jale la linea, por favor!*" I said. He grabbed a line. The wrong line.

"*¡No! ¡El otro! ¡El verde!*" I pointed at the green one.

"*¡No! ¡A la otra moda!*" I told him to pull it in the other direction.

He was totally confused, and my Spanish was too limited to explain the intricate workings of a sailboat — a difficult enough task in English — so I took the line and showed him how to pull it in and cleat it as the boat rocked back and forth in the waves and water sloshed aboard. After that, he very happily left all the linehandling to me — which was just as well for both of us. He settled back on the starboard seat with his head safely below the boom, and happily watched the coastline pass by.

"*¡Que bonito es!*" he summed up the entire experience of simply being out upon the water with no gasoline smell and no powerboat noise, with only the sound of the sails and the slap of the waves to accompany us. We were out there with the sea and the birds sailing past that red volcanic headland. It was indeed beautiful.

I brought her about and beached her again, and Jesus said yet again what a beautiful experience it had been for him. Then as he "helped" us put her back on the trailer and take down the mast, he explained to Carolyn that this was the first time he had ever been out in a sailboat. In fact, she translated, he had never even been out in a boat of any kind before. And to think that an American would take him out there in his boat! It was beyond belief! He was so excited I thought he might pee his pants, and he kept saying "*!Gracias, señor! ¡Muchas gracias!*" as we put the boat away and headed to dinner.

It was a wonderful, and memorable, first day for all of us aboard our little boat on the Sea of Cortez. She was now part of the family.

It was time to name her.

Naming a little boat has serious implications that I'm sure you'll understand, Eliot. There are ship naming ceremonies that have been developed over many centuries by those familiar with the notoriously unpredictable nature of the Gods

---

Bahia de Kino

of the sea. Ancient mariners invested much thought in this very serious matter that requires one to appease the Sea Gods, because a mistake in the ceremony can have dire consequences for anyone who may be so foolish, or rash, as to dismiss such an important matter as superstition. It's a very serious matter, Eliot, and I'm sure you would agree. I'm not willing to take a chance angering Poseidon, or Neptune, or certainly Proteus, the father of all the ancient gods.

But these are gods with more important things to do than to waste time wreaking mischief on a couple of properly respectful sailors in a small boat. They have much larger, and more presumptuous, vessels to deal with out there far beyond the horizon. Many are corporate-owned and see the treasures of the ocean as commodities to be taken at will and sold to the highest bidder. Others use the oceans for transport and the winds and waves are not the means of their passage, like the schooners and dhows and tall square-riggers of old, but only a nuisance and impediment to motorized progress. They don't properly respect the sea, the weather, and the ancient gods.

Yes, the Sea Gods have much other, and well-justified, mischief to attend to. They can't be overly bothered with us.

Yet they still demand a certain measure of respect, if we hope to gain their benign forbearance. They demand that we respect the moods of the sea and that we do nothing foolish that may require their intervention in our favor. These are busy gods, and they can't be bothered often with requests for a sudden favorable wind to drive a capsized small boat onto a soft and sandy beach. We must take personal responsibility so as not to demand such favors of the Sea Gods — at least not often. As responsible mariners, there may come a day when we'll need their assistance. Then they'll be much more likely to listen to our frantic prayers.

And there are certain other things which must be part of any ceremony that asks not only the forbearance of the gods, but which might presume to ask their blessing, and maybe even a measure of protection whenever we have dared to venture forth into their watery realm. An uncovered head and a respectful voice are essential parts of the ceremony. I'll keep that in mind as I ask their permission, and their acceptance, in the naming of this small and inconsequential craft that presumes to embark upon their broad and mighty waters.

These gods rule the frozen waters of the Arctic, the towering waves of the North Pacific, the stormy waters of the Atlantic. Yet they are the same gods who rule the warm and gentle seas of the South Pacific, the Caribbean, and even the Sea of Cortez — although they send an occasional hurricane to remind us of their powers when the waters get too warm, and we get too complacent. Last week, we met with their messenger, Hurricane Juliette, and she reminded us not to take the Sea Gods too lightly. We assured her that we would give much serious thought to the process of naming this little boat and, although she is gone now, we fully intend to keep our promise lest another member of her family comes to pay us a visit.

Another important aspect of a boat-naming ceremony is the offering of something dear. Offering a big brother to be taken away by the Sea Gods as a galley slave is not considered an appropriate gift, as there may be a bit too much joy on the part of the little brother. Rather, the gift must require a measure of sacrifice on the part of the giver. This requires serious thought on our part. It must be something acceptable to the gods, something they will wish to grace their beautiful sea. We will give it much careful consideration lest we do something egregious to offend them.

And it is important to remember that, despite their being Lords of a Watery Realm, the Sea Gods are thirsty sods. The pirates and seafarers of long ago knew these gods require a dram of decent grog with each entreaty for their blessing. On the Irish coast, this would be a glass of fine Irish whisky. Along the Spanish Main, a flask of good Jamaican rum. And here, on the sun-washed shores of the Sea of Cortez, a snifter of fine Mexican brandy would be most appropriate. There's a bottle of Don Pedro on the shelf, and Carolyn and I will each volunteer to enjoy a sip, solely to assure the gods that it is a worthy and acceptable offering, you understand. And, if you were here, I'd sneak a sip in your direction — while your parents were otherwise occupied — to gain the Sea Gods' full blessing upon you, my friend, as well.

With all that in mind, I'll work to compose a proper naming ceremony for this sweet little sailing craft over the next few days, and we'll name her here where we took our first sail together. I'll get back to you when we're ready.

And, after all the important issues that are part of this solemn ceremony, there's still another consideration attached to our naming of this small sailboat after you, my very young departed nephew. It means that I could never sell her to anyone else, and that was one of the main reasons for our taking her out upon the sea today. It was important that we spend the time to know her well, and that we are comfortable with each other — her with us, and we with her.

As you know well, we have owned a number of sailboats over the years, ranging from a very traditional small craft built on the eastern shore, through several small boats that I built in the garage as tenders for Liberación, our lovely 25-footer, that you spent time aboard over the years on a warm lake in southern New

Bahia de Kino

Mexico. We have developed a familiarity with small craft and their temperaments, and not all of them have suited us well.

But this one, this small craft that we'll now name Elioto, took good care of us today on the benign and breezy waters of the Sea of Cortez, and I know that I would feel comfortable taking other young nephews and nieces out in her to experience the sea. A boat as sea-kindly as this fine lady would give little reason to sell her at some point in the future.

And that has to be the mark of a fine little sailboat.

A Little Octopus Stranded on the Beach

October 12, 2001

Dear Eliot,

This morning at dawn the sun slanted across the Sea of Cortez, and it touched everything with a glow of brilliant orange. Right offshore, and just outside our bedroom window, the birds were circling and diving from about thirty feet above the water into a large school of fish. There were so many birds that they looked like a swam of bees circling in the air. When they dived, the horizontal rays of the morning sun caught their white bellies and they looked like white missiles assaulting the sea, each one leaving a fountain of white spray in its wake.

Closer in, a large fish made passes through that same school of little fish. At each pass, the surface swirled and small fish leapt from the water in panic. The sun flashed against their silvery sides for a brief moment before they fell back into the embrace of the sea.

It's about 8:30 a.m. now, and we've finished breakfast. As we look out at this constantly fascinating ocean, the bows of the shrimp boats are pointed toward the harbor. The horizon is speckled with boats motoring in to unload their nightly catch. We scan the sea with binoculars and see their nets hanging and swaying as each boat plows onward through the water. And in the quiet of the morning, we can just hear the drone of heavy diesel engines throbbing their way home for the day.

Every morning the sea begins this timeless ritual in much the same way.

Yesterday afternoon we went for a long walk eastward, barefoot, down the beach. In the afternoon sun, the wet volcanic sand had the look of thick and

---

Bahia de Kino

silky milk chocolate beneath our feet. There were new shells, different shells, lying upon the silky sand, as there always are each time we walk the beach. There were special shells to put beside the ones that grace the seawall at our rented house, and we planned to gather them on the way back, if someone else hadn't done so already.

We disturbed a large group of pelicans and gulls that had convened to digest their daily catch, while they enjoyed the beauty of another sunset on the desert sea. They flew out over the water as we approached and returned to the beach after we passed.

We walked into a heavy concentration of broken shells and rocks, and we stepped carefully through them. The shells clattered in the surf as it crashed over the rounded volcanic rocks that may have made their way inshore from Isla Pelicano over the centuries. It is possible that this area of rocks and broken shells is the grinding area that generates the sand we walk on.

On our way back, we found a small octopus lying dazed, but alive, on the sand. I know you would have loved to see him, Eliot. Tentacles and all, he was about the size of my hand — although I didn't feel like shaking hands with him, if you know what I mean. Where do you even start to shake hands with an octopus, anyway? He looked up to us from the sand with doleful eyes, as if he was sad. And maybe he was afraid, too, as he looked up at two huge creatures peering down at him. And him just stuck there, helpless, on the sand. There was a plastic bottle with the end cut off lying on the sand nearby, so I scooped up some water to splash over him. He seemed to respond to that. He sucked in some of the water, and spit it back out.

I got some more water and poured it over him and he drank it in again. And then I scooped him up along with a bunch of water and sand, and I waded out into the ocean to let him go. But that wasn't as easy as I thought it might be. He decided to grab hold of the inside of the bottle with his suction cups, and I couldn't dump him out. I tried to wash him out, but he just held on tighter. I held up the bottle, full of water now, and looked at him in there sloshing around happily in his element. And he looked back at me. He needed to go back to the sea where he belonged. And we needed to go home.

I didn't want to throw the plastic bottle out into the ocean, so I picked up a long beautiful pointed shell from the beach and I began to pry him gently from the bottle. But, as soon as I had one tentacle loose, he'd grab hold with another one. I worked more quickly. Finally I pried him completely loose from the plastic bottle and he grabbed onto the shell. I tossed him back into the sea, tightly

---

I Always Meant to Tell You...

grasping the shell, and watched him disappear in the swirling surf. Then I stepped out of the sea and onto the land. Each of us was back where he belonged, and the sun was setting.

It was time to go home.

Bahia de Kino

El Barquito de Velas Elioto

October 12, 2001

Dearest Eliot,

    This afternoon we listened to a CD of ancient sea shanties sung by the 97th Regimental Band as we looked out onto a beautiful blue sea covered with whitecaps — white ponies galloping forever over the oceans of the world. All we need to complete this scene of enduring and surpassing beauty is for a full-rigged ship to pull round the headland out there beyond Pelican Island. This bay a sight that the salty tars who shipped out of gray, overcast ports in England and along the northeastern American seaboard, dreamt of when they signed aboard ships heading south to warmer seas. And here we stand, with the gift of looking out across this rare and remote stretch of water.

    Sea shanties are about hauling lines, raising sails, and leaving loved ones behind. When the ships returned, there was rejoicing and merriment — and the enjoyment of a fine beverage or two. I know you'd have seen the humor in these songs and could imagine a tallship pulling into the bay, her crew ready for shore leave. They'd drop a heavy anchor well offshore and let the bow of their ship swing up into the wind. After she was riding well to her anchor, and all was secure, they'd lower the shore boats and there would be a mad scramble for the lucky ones to get aboard. Then, about six men in each boat would bend their backs to the oars as the coxswain called out a rhythm, and they'd race for shore where they'd drag the boats up beyond the high water mark before setting out for some entertainment. It would indeed be a sight to behold.

    And as we look out upon the beautiful Sea of Cortez this afternoon, it's an easy sight to imagine, Eliot. I wish you were here to enjoy it.

Bahia de Kino

But the reason I'm writing today is to let you know that I believe I have a proper ceremony for the Sea Gods so they will allow us to name that little sailboat you and I picked out a few months back. Maybe they'll grant us their protection as we venture out upon their seas. It's taken me several days of thought, and I hope it's acceptable for the occasion.

The people of every seagoing culture have prayed to their Sea Gods whenever they embarked upon the broad oceans of the world. Ancient Phoenicians prayed to their gods as they explored unknown waters beyond the horizon. Ancient Arabs prayed before embarking in their dhows on voyages of discovery. Norsemen prayed to their gods before they left in longboats to discover a New World that lay far to the west. The whalers of New Bedford prayed to their god to bring them and their tallships home safely from the sea.

There are so many gods that it's hard to know what to say to them. Frankly, I have always found this god stuff to be very confusing. Still, it's appropriate that we say something to a higher power or two before we dare to embark upon the sea. So here is what I'll say this evening while Carolyn and I stand upon the shore as the sun sets once more over the beautiful Sea of Cortez:

> *Oh Great Proteus, father of the ancient classical gods;*
> *Oh Great Poseidon, ancient Greek God of the Sea;*
> *Oh Great Neptune, ancient Roman God of the Sea;*
> *Oh Great Hant Caai, ancient God of the Seri people*
>   *who've lived on this shore since time began:*
> *Please grant us our petition to name this humble craft in honor of one who*
>   *has fallen, and who cannot be with us here today.*
> *Please accept the name of Elioto for this small vessel.*
> *On his behalf, please accept this small boat upon your waters and please*
>   *protect her as she makes her way throughout your Glorious Watery Realm.*
> *You have much work to do in tending the oceans and you can't waste time*
>   *on the troubles of foolish souls like us who ply your seas in small craft.*
> *So we assure you that our intentions are pure and that we will respect the*
>   *moods and the power of your creation, the beautiful sea, whenever we*
>   *embark upon her.*
> *We likewise assure you that we will act responsibly and will endeavor not*
>   *to require your intervention on our behalf.*

Please grant us safe passage as we learn from and celebrate your magnificent oceans and those who dwell within them, upon them, and along their margins.
We promise not to test your powers irresponsibly, now or in the future.
Please accept our small gift and a full measure of fine Mexican brandy, of which we will share a glass with you this fine evening, as simple tokens of our appreciation of your great works, and the great reverence in which we hold your beautiful creation, the Sea of Cortez.
Thank you for your benevolence and your kindness toward us, and may we always be worthy of your trust as we venture forth upon your waters.

And so, Eliot, on the evening of October 12, 2001, I stood at the sandy edge of the ocean and recited these words to the Sea Gods at the water lapped against my bare feet. Then Carolyn and I each drank a bit of fine Mexican brandy from a hand-blown chalice and poured the rest into the Sea of Cortez as a gift to the gods. As a final gesture, I threw a beautiful golden 20-peso coin far out into the embrace of the sea.

Now Eliot, whenever I sail our little boat, I'll always sail her with you.

Bahia de Kino

The Restaurant Marlyn

October 13, 2001

Dear Steve,

    Last night, we went to the restaurant Marlyn in Kino Viejo. Sammy, their excellent chef, was still there. You would remember him, although he may not remember all the many faces he's seen over the years at the tables of the Marlyn. We had hoped that there would be music last night, but the musicians don't start playing until next week, after more of the snowbirds arrive in their RVs from as far away as Canada and Alaska.

    A few years back, our family walked from Saro's to Old Kino in the glorious colors of another sunset. It was a little farther than most of us thought, so we were very hungry when we finally walked through the door. There were nine of us, and we filled that long table to the left. First of all, a round of margaritas was in order, along with baskets of chips.

    As we placed our orders, a man with a very good voice played the guitar and sang the songs we requested. When we ran out of choices, he sang very good selections of his own.

    During a lull, I beckoned him to my end of the table. He bent to listen as I said, *"Mira el hombre al otro lado de la mesa."*

    He looked at the far end of the table where you were sitting, and he nodded. You had a suspicious look, and a wry smile, as you wondered what I was up to this time.

    "El hombre allá canta muy bien 'De Colores'." I said.

    "¿Oh, sí?" he replied.

    He went to your end of the table and handed you the guitar. It was your turn

Bahía de Kino

to sing for the lucky customers who happened to be at the Marlyn that night. To the surprise of everyone there, the whole family joined in as you sang the song we knew so well, the one we'd heard you sing many times before.

Now I don't know if a round of De Colores, well played and well sung to a small crowd one night long ago in the Restaurant Marlyn in Bahia de Kino Viejo, counts as an "International Engagement" in the register where they keep track of such things, Steve, but it always will to me.

I'm still proud of you.

Goodbye, Steve

October 19, 2001

And so now our time on this forgotten shore has come to an end. Tomorrow we leave our refuge by the sea and return to a world that won't allow us to escape, not just yet.

We've spent our time here in solitude looking for escape, but looking for answers as well, answers to what are destined to remain unanswerable questions. We now know the answers will never come, and the dull and constant pain will never leave. Surely, I will take these questions to my grave.

It's time now to think of your son, Alec, and of his grandparents, and of Eliot's many cousins with fascinating lives of their own as they continue to explore their own corners of this vast world.

It's time to leave the questions behind, for now.

Yet there's another question, a rhetorical question, if you will.

Why Kino Bay? In fact, why Mexico? Why was it so important to spend this time on the shore of this particular sea?

Yes, in the wake of the accident, I had an undeniable need to escape the mindless distractions of the world. All my life, escape has been a constant desire of mine. You know that very well about me. But let me try to explain why we came south, beyond the border.

Mexico has had an allure for me, and for you as well, since we were kids buying cheap knives, bullwhips, plaster skulls and all those bizarre trinkets that a couple of ten- and twelve-year-old gringo kids could find in the tourist shops that lined the main street in Ciudad Juarez back in the 1950s. And who could forget those packages of "Bullshit Cigarettes." Really. That's what it said right across the

---

Bahia de Kino

front of each package, and down the side: Bullshit Cigarettes. I don't know if that's what was in them, really, but every shop had a wide, shallow basket filled with those little packages. It was just inside the door. You and I were both tempted to buy a pack — they were only 10 cents each, as I recall — to show our friends when we got back to Alburquerque. But neither of us had the nerve to try sneaking it back under the watchful eyes of our parents. Imagine if one of those little packages had somehow turned up in our stuff. Neither of us could lie our way out of a situation like that. We'd have caught hell.

It was a very different and exotic world for a couple of gringo kids back then, and it was only a day's drive south from where we lived.

And in the early seventies, I took long trips by bus throughout Mexico, or as far as I could get until the money ran out. In those days it really was possible to travel in Mexico on "five and ten dollars a day," as long as you didn't travel like a tourist. I could live with that. I traveled on funky old buses with animals tied to the roof on their way to market, and I stayed in hotels that Mexican travelers stayed in. I have to admit it was more interesting, at times, than I would have preferred, but I got through it alright and I learned a few things along the way.

That was never your style, Steve, finding yourself alone at night in the deserted streets of a foreign city looking for a hotel, although you were always fascinated by the stories I told whenever I managed to survive another trip beyond the border. And how much of this adventuring was just an effort to get a rise out of an impressionable little brother? Jeez, I don't know, Steve. Probably some of it; maybe most of it. I don't know. When we were both younger, you often had a look of amazed disapproval on your face whenever I told you of my latest adventure. And I'd embellish it a bit to make sure I got that reaction from you. Still, I think you always wished you'd taken some more exotic adventures too.

I guess we're going to have to leave it there, now. That's destined to be another one of those cosmic unanswered questions. Dammit.

Later, we learned to appreciate each other for our experiences, and to see the good in what the other had done. And frankly, Steve, now that I've gotten a little older and maybe a little softer, and now that I have a little more money in my pocket, I tend to look for places that are less funky and more comfortable to spend my time in — places that even you would enjoy. And I have a fellow adventurer now to explore this fascinating country with. She often surprises me by suggesting places to stay that might look a little undesirable on the surface, but then turn out to be fine. That comes from her Peace Corps background, and it causes me to wonder if people join the Peace Corps because they're adventurous, or if that's the way they end up. Chicken and egg stuff, you know.

Janette was like that, wasn't she? She went into exotic situations and didn't waste much time worrying about it, about whether she was going to be comfortable or not. She worked things out when she got there, and she probably dragged you into some surprising situations that turned out to be good for you, didn't she? I can imagine her doing that.

The fact is, there are many different experiences in Mexico. There are many different Mexicans, just as there are *norteamericanos*; they're all people like you and me. I've found that to be true of every culture I've encountered. Some people are pedantic and efficient. They're the ones who make the buses run on time, well mostly. Others are hopelessly romantic, and they add art and beauty to our lives. Those are the ones we most enjoy searching out and spending our time with — not some expatriate bridge-playing gringo community of people who make no effort to learn the language and rub shoulders with the locals. Life's too short to waste it in predictable mediocrity.

But this year was different. We didn't need an adventure this year. We needed to escape, pure and simple.

We have been to Bahia de Kino many times over the past decade and we have always found the escape we were seeking. There is an undeniable attraction to simply being away, for a month, from the distractions of telephone, television, and the Internet — that latest collection of electronic inanity that keeps us from being full citizens of the natural world in which we live.

If we really need to make a phone call, there's a public phone about a block away. The idea that people would be unable to call us directly was a deliciously attractive option. We're also insulated from hysterical media reports of the mindless conflict that seems to engulf the world these days. The Hermosillo newspaper only carries a fraction of that stuff.

Yes, Steve, that's the latent Luddite in me rising to the surface again. It's always there, just beneath a veneer of societal respectability, and waiting to assault any new idea with the well-honed weapons of skepticism. Call me a modern disciple (a impertinent concept, don't you think?) of Ned Lud, the English artisan of the early 1800s who led a rebellion against the machinery that was stealing jobs and destroying the ancient trades. He failed, and I will too, in my railings against the "progress" of our modern age. Yet it seems good to do this, and not to accept without question the clever rascals who hold profit foremost like a sacred flambeau, who ensure their own enrichment at the expense of the rest. No, I prefer to remain among the outcasts, the infidel iconoclasts.

You know it well, that trait of mine. We discussed it often, you who always embraced the new, I who was always reluctant. We were each a test of the other's ideas, although not our ideals, which we held in common and which we discussed again as we walked these sandy shores in the many (which now seem precious few) evenings available when we were here together.

Now that I've been here for a month of quiet and reflection, there are reasons besides escapism to return to this sleepiest of villages by the sea. This is the last place where you and I had the time, a considerable amount of time, to really talk to each other. There were young children around with excited questions about this new world they were discovering for themselves, experienced each moment through perceptive young eyes. They needed us to explore it with them. And we did, as fascinated with each new, and beautiful, shell as they were. Yet there was still time, to talk of many things as we swam in this benevolent sea and we walked along this seven-mile crescent beach — which can seem almost endless, when you really want it to be, or need it to be. I felt that we had only begun to rediscover a rich vein that we could mine forever, someday, when we had the time.

It is the custom of men to talk obliquely about their feelings by discussing sports, fishing, work, and other things. Those are the ways in which we define ourselves, the ways in which we give value to our lives. And in manly conversations, we speak in ways that make it appear as if any discussion of values and feelings is somehow stumbled into by accident. It is not our custom to talk in depth about our feelings. And when we find ourselves mired in such uncomfortable terrain, we backtrack quickly to safer territory. It's just how we are.

Yet I was hoping to engage in real conversation with you at some point in the not too distant future, after you and I had each attained a reasonable economic base for our old age and for our dependents. I was hoping that you and I could actually sit with a glass of brandy (my preference), or go for a long walk (your preference), and discuss where each of us planned to go from here, now that we actually had the freedom. I cannot imagine that either of us would "go quietly into that dark night" that lies endless before us as we grow old. I wanted to hear, not about your latest dealings with some corporate board — although I always found that stuff interesting — but about what you may have learned so far, the principles of your work, your plans to write down some of this to add to the body of human knowledge. And what you planned to do with it afterwards. I felt you had so much to offer.

I Always Meant to Tell You...

You always provided for other people. You managed to provide for the needs of others and make them feel comfortable in your presence. You did it gracefully, without condescension, because you genuinely felt concerned about the needs of others — especially the members of your own family. I always envied your ability to do that, and I hoped someday to be able to provide some greater measure of service to others than I have been able to in the past. It was not my way, but it was a skill I was hoping to learn some day, from you.

There is so much that I still wanted to talk to you about, and I imagined much of it happening here in quiet Kino Bay when we were able to step away from our commercial lives and let someone else have a chance at that elusive brass ring. When we were finally able to come here and make this place our home, a place of refuge for our family and our many friends. A simple and quiet place for each of us to spend long hours at peace.

And now, there's an end to it. Now it's been said.

Our long walks and quiet talks can never happen here — at least not in the way I had imagined them. Yet I think that you and I will take long walks on this ancient beach forever, in late afternoon, as the Sonoran desert sun retreats in its final blazing moments behind distant Isla Tiburon and paints the sea once more in golds and reds. I know that you and I — and Janette, and Eliot — will be together now forever.

And if a passing person should see an aging fellow in a worn straw hat walking in the shallow surf at sunset, and if he seems to be conversing with himself, or perhaps he seems lost in an endless conversation with someone yet unseen, I would hope that passerby would have the decency not to notice a tear upon the old man's cheek, and to walk on by in silence.

Bahia de Kino

PART IV

Afterwords
Alburquerque, New Mexico

A Roll of Photographs

Late October, 2001

Dear Steve,

Your photographs arrived today. The ones you took on the hike to those curious rock formations called granite tors, and later at the lake just before your plane lifted from the water's surface for the last time. A small film canister was found at the crash site; and Nancy's husband, Hugh, had it developed. Although we can never know for certain whose camera it came from, I'm sure it was yours because you always took pictures to document family moments.

I recall that the well known New Mexico photographer, Harvey Caplin, once inquired about a large picture of yours that he saw in a rack at the place where you had them developed. You were just an amateur, and he didn't recognize your name. "Not bad," is all he said before returning to his own work. The clerk said he mentioned it to you because Caplin is notoriously economical with his compliments. Notice from someone like Caplin is worth sharing, and I was very impressed when you told me.

In the very last picture, you're standing on the banks of Lake Sithylemenkat, looking out over the quiet waters, taking in the beauty of the vast Alaskan wilderness, and marveling at your incredible young son who's actually swimming in that frigid lake. The sky is a light and gentle blue and there are just a few puffy white clouds floating overhead. In the distance, richly covered hills of scrub forest and brush rise gradually from lake "Sithy" and recede toward distant blue mountains. You're surrounded by thousands of square miles of fertile roadless habitat, home to deer, elk, bear, and moose and a silence punctuated only briefly when a small float plane came into view and landed on these deep

---

Bahia de Kino

still waters. It was a perfect sunny day for a hike to the rocks and for a bit of blueberry picking.

Nancy is standing proudly beside her shiny white and red plane in that last picture, as it faces outward to the lake. Its long pontoons are pulled up to the sandy shore by a line tied to the tree you're standing by. There's something compelling about float planes. They occupy an undeniably romantic space in the imagination that is reserved for adventure in vast exotic places beyond where the roads end. There isn't a soul in our family who doesn't understand the call of that unmarked sky road that each of you chose to travel that day to your destiny.

Eliot is shoulder-deep in cold lake water in the foreground of that last picture, enjoying a swim after hiking through the hills. For Eliot, the lure of diving into cold lake water would be a powerful temptation after a hike under the afternoon sun. He spent most of each winter in a t-shirt, without a coat. You must have grimaced as he leapt into that icy water, and in the picture you still wear the vestige of a wry smile. I would have grimaced, too. We tall skinny types have a natural aversion to cold water. We both envied Eliot's ability to shrug off the coldest weather and dive fully into whatever faced him.

Janette took that last picture on the roll, and it remains as the poignant conclusion to a pictorial record of a beautiful afternoon spent exploring the northern boundaries of the world in grand and simple style. A robust and wonderful way to experience life to its fullest and richest.

As the afternoon moved on, the warm arctic summer sun gave little indication that the hour was growing late. Still, it was time to go. Time for a long flight back to Fairbanks, time to put the plane away, time to make dinner. Hugh was waiting at home. At last, it was time to load your gear. In just a few more minutes you would board Nancy's plane, strap on your seat belts, and fly off forever into a blue Alaskan sky.

That's how I hope to remember the moment.

NOTE: See selection of photographs in Appendix.

Eliot's School

November 1, 2001
Alburquerque, New Mexico

Dear Eliot,

Your school called today.

Sarah Anaya called from Alameda Elementary School to tell me the students had written letters and collected money in your memory. The money will be donated to a fund to help the people who lost their loved ones in the New York City airliner crashes. It's a tremendously nice thing for them to do.

I recall the day I went to your school on Parents Day, when Steve was out of town. I took the morning off from work, picked you up at your house, and took you to school. It was a good experience to see how well you got along with the other kids and how much fun you were to be with. You were a bright spot for the class, and they enjoyed joking around with you. And you were a good example of how to add constructively to the class and still have fun doing it. I'm very glad you gave me the opportunity to go with you that day. I'll always remember it.

They have plans to install a plaque at the school with your name on it. I'll visit the plaque quietly now, and then after it's on the wall, because I want to maintain contact with you. This seems like a way I can do that.

I don't know what people are supposed to do when they find themselves in a situation like this. I suppose everyone confronted with this kind of thing develops a special way to deal with it. I feel so clumsy, and inarticulate, and inadequate. Yet I don't know that there's any way to deal with this elegantly and as a matter of course. That simply doesn't seem possible.

Eliot, for what it's worth, I just want you to know that I miss you.

A Year Later

October 10, 2002
Bahia de Kino, Mexico

Dear Steve,

    We have returned to Kino Bay a year later on our usual September pilgrimage. The water is warm as it always is at this time of the year, generating *las tormentas*, the thunderstorms that sweep inland to water the parched deserts of Sonora, Arizona, and New Mexico. And hurricanes like the one we faced the day after we arrived last year. We drove through heavy rains after we crossed the border, but so far there's no sign of a hurricane this year.

    It's been over a year since your death in Alaska and I still can't really believe it's true. It still seems so incomprehensible to me — that there's a gate somewhere that keeps us apart. I wish that I could touch your hand, if only for a moment, and we could talk about all that's happened since you left. But I know it can never be, that's what the rational and mature side of me is trying to tell my primitive atavistic side. These emotions struggle each day for ascendancy, and I'm torn by battles raging within. In the end, there's only a dull pain to deal with, as best I can.

    Our trip south to the border is yet another passage of remembrance — painful at times, joyful at others — as we remember all that each of you meant to us. We stopped for dinner again at the Stage Stop Inn in Patagonia, Arizona; and this time we stayed for the night. It's not far from the border, and we planned to cross early the next day. You liked its funky, corny, cowboy decor. You were more tolerant of that sort of thing than I ever was. In Nogales, we passed that little motel near the border where we all stayed for the night and cooled off in the pool in anticipation of being in the Sea of Cortez in another day.

Afterwords

But this year, the border was closed on the Mexican side by protesters outraged at the high electric bills they received this past month. We had at least another day ahead of us in Arizona so we did something neither of us ever does at home. We stopped at a Walmart to get some items we left behind in our rush to pack.

Spanish is very handy at any store in Nogales, and it's a good way to find out things that remain hidden to those bound by a single tongue. We asked a young clerk about the protest, and she was very familiar with it. She lives on the Mexican side of the border, and her electric bill for the previous month was more than $200 — double what ours was for three small homes and one business in our little Alburquerque compound. We can't imagine how she pays a bill like that working for minimum wage at Walmart. After a night in a hotel near the bypass route, we crossed early before the protests were expected to resume.

In Hermosillo, we stopped again at Sanborn's where we ate lunch together three years ago. And nearing Kino Bay, we passed that large, forgotten masonry gateway that still stands on the south side of the road. It still has *"¡Luchamos por una casa para estudiantes!"* scrawled across it. Like so many other grand and unfinished projects throughout Mexico, it reminds me of Yeats' poem, "Ozymandias," about two legs of stone standing alone in the desert.

But I mention the old gateway because it's where Carolyn waited by the car for someone to bring us gasoline. My little Nissan Sentra wagon got such great mileage that I forgot to check the gas gauge before we left Hermosillo. And yet again as we passed the Pemex station in Miguel Alemán. I was reminded as we rolled to a stop near the abandoned gateway in the desert — about 10 kilometers short of Bahia de Kino. We stood by the road while the rest of you went ahead to the Hotel Saro where our rooms were waiting.

Soon, you and Saro arrived with a plastic milk carton full of gas, and we poured it into the tank. Then you and I paused for a moment while we tried to figure out what to do with the empty container. I didn't want it smelling up the car, but there was no other place to put it. Then Saro said *"¡Tirela!* " (Just throw it!), and he swept his hand toward a desert already filled with trash. Steve, I remember you and me looking into each other's eyes for a sign, a suggestion, a way to soothe our liberal gringo sensibilities. There was none, and so I reluctantly tossed the empty plastic milk carton into a cluttered desert and drove onward to Kino Bay.

I felt guilty and I hoped that somewhere in that Great Karmic Book, where they keep a record of these things, it would be duly noted that we had added to the general clutter of Mexico only as unwilling outsiders for lack of an alternative. I believe it's generally a good thing for Americans to go along with prevailing customs, and not to try to impose our culture on the world. Yet, I have a very hard time disregarding the environment no matter what the locals custom, and you felt the same way. You and I, and the rest of our family, picked trash off the beach each day for the rest of the week in atonement for our brief moment of sin.

So, I think you'd like to know that a few things have changed since the year we came to Kino together. There was a huge volunteer trash pickup last year on the day we had to leave for home. We found out about it just as we were driving out, and we promised to help next year. I don't know if it's a result of these efforts, but the entire area seems to look a little better this year than it did before. And, Steve, I think you would appreciate the positive incremental change.

But a few other things have changed here, too. The funky old Hotel Saro is no more. Saro's dilapidated old building is still there, but the sign is gone. And so is Saro. Our friend Maria told us he gave up trying to sell the place and moved into Hermosillo. Most of the people who come here now want a higher level of comfort than that offered by the old Mexico. They've gotten used to better things; and they have the money to pay for higher quality, especially air-conditioning. Maria said the hotel is now rented to a group that might use it as a school for wayward kids, like the one that now occupies the Anchor House. As far as I know, Saro's was the last cheap place to stay that was right on the beach.

This morning we ate breakfast on the terraza. We worked on a *crucigrama* (crossword puzzle) from the Hermosillo paper until the heat drove us to our bathing suits. The sea was warm but refreshing, and we found ourselves in the midst of a school of small fish in its morning cruise down the coast. Alfredo calls them *chuchillos*, and he says they're very tasty fried in oil. They're a reliable food source for the gulls and pelicans and the larger fish. Waves of small silvery fish leap from the water when a big fish sweeps through the school for a mouthful. This morning, large green crabs with beautiful blue legs and little schools of small dark fish feed in the shallows. Life in this warm sea goes on as it has for years uncountable.

Still, Mexico is changing, Steve. It's very different from our days as young kids buying cheap knives, bullwhips, and other trinkets in the colorful *Mercado Principal* in Ciudad Juarez. And it's different than the 1970s when I used to travel by bus deep into the interior. Disturbing poverty still remains, but there's a

Afterwords

younger generation working for a better life than their parents had, and that's a hopeful sign for this nation's future. Carolyn and I are at ease in Mexico, as we watch the dynamic changes that ripple through this rich culture.

I'm just very sorry that you, and Janette, and Eliot can never return to experience with us again all that this fascinating country can offer.

The Dream

November 1, 2002
Alburquerque, New Mexico

Dear Steve,

    I just can't tell you how wonderful it was to see you last night, when you visited my dreams.
    I thought I would never have another chance to see you, to talk with you quietly about all that has happened since you died. To share so many of those feelings that we never seemed to have time for when you were here. You looked very nice in that brown suit you were wearing, a suit I don't remember ever having seen before. That's how things often are in dreams, though.
    I don't remember much detail about our surroundings, about the place where we were sitting, except we appeared to be sitting on a stone wall in a quiet pastoral setting. We sat quietly and savored those few minutes we'd been granted again of each other's company, and I felt we both wished we'd spent more time that way when we could have. It meant so much to me just to sit with you and tell you how sorry I am that you're gone now. I had never fully appreciated you while you were alive, although I was coming to realize your importance to me when you died. Your death robbed me of the opportunity to share that with you.
    You sat and listened and then you nodded your head, in acceptance more than resignation, and I felt that you knew I'd do my best with what's left here to me. Your presence, temporary though it was, filled me with a feeling of reassurance that I've needed for some time now.
    And then it was time for you to go. Something called to you, a voice unheard by me. We both stood and embraced for just a moment longer. And that moment

felt unlike an ending, but more like a beginning to the next part of our life-long relationship, like a joyful interlude in the continuum of two lives that will remain forever inter-twined.

There was no sense of sorrow or finality to the moment as I knew somehow you and I would return to this place and this time often in the future.

And that we'd share these moments until the day I die.

Epilogue

Lunes, 22 de septiembre del 2003
Bahia de Kino, Sonora

And so Steve, in the Fall of 2003, we return to Kino Bay.

As the nights grow longer and the intense heat of a very long summer finally begins to wane, we head southwest again through the heart of the Chihuahuan and Sonoran deserts. We pass the human habitations and the natural places along the Interstate that have now become so familiar through the years we've made this trip. And finally we reach the Mexican border.

I don't know how to explain it, but I've begun to feel that this may be our next home. Perhaps it's the sheer primal beauty of this desert sea, and the cultural solitude that comes with it; perhaps that's what pulls me so strongly. I have an increasing fascination with these people and their rich heritage. I know Carolyn shares that fascination, she's so curious and always open to new experience.

We finish our paperwork at the entry point about twenty-one kilometers below the border. It took on a new dimension this year when someone lifted Carolyn's handbag containing all her ID, with the exception of her passport. They also got my duffel with my clothes in it. But all that stuff is replaceable, and they probably need it more than we do. Life goes on.

We head south, through small and simple towns that have now become familiar to us. At Imuris, a narrow winding mountain road leads east toward Cananea, where miners were once massacred for demanding decent pay. We've driven that road. At Magdalena de Kino, the highway serpentines through the sahuaro forest that surrounds the town. The tall white *iglesia* built under the direction of Padre Kino stands as a beacon for the devout. The Padre is buried there. At Santa Ana, we'll stop for a cold soda again, perhaps a meal, at the Restaurant Elba before heading down the long straight toll road through the desert to Hermosillo.

We need to be in Hermosillo on Tuesday to pick up Carolyn's daughter, Cici, at the airport. She's coming in from Oakland via Southwest Airlines to Phoenix, and from there she'll catch an Aeromexico flight to Hermosillo. She's bringing a supply of Peet's Coffee with her as a special treat. It's the first time we've had a family member join us at the house, and we're looking forward to her visit. She'll be staying with us for a week.

Again, as we have for the past five years or so, we rented the home at 5665 Mar de Cortez with its broad terraza opening directly out to the sea. It's just half a block west of the Hotel Saro where we all stayed for Mom's seventieth birthday. This nice home, a mansion really, by our standards, has become our annual refuge from the grim realities of the world.

We wish we had been able to share this special place with you, Steve, and with your family.

There's no phone and no TV. There's an excellent AM station broadcasting classical music and other programs from the Universidad de Sonora in Hermosillo. We buy the local newspaper, *El Imparcial*, that comes from Hermosillo. It's a fairly thick newspaper that only carries about a page of news concerning the US. The rest is coverage of local events, the news of Mexico, and important events around the world. That seems like the right proportion. It's refreshing to leave behind the self-absorbed world of the US for a while. Maybe someday we'll leave it forever.

Once again, there's a hurricane warning on the front page of *El Imparcial*. The Sunday morning headlines read, *"Va 'Marty' a Peninsula."* Hurricane Marty has formed in the Pacific a few hundred miles west of Guadalajara, and it's headed north toward the southern tip of Baja California, a frequent landfall for Mexican hurricanes. After it comes ashore on Monday afternoon, it's projected to cross the peninsula and head toward northern Sonora, just like Julieta did two years ago, just after we arrived. Julieta was a very interesting experience for two inlanders who had never dealt with hurricanes before. Even the word "hurricane" strikes fear into most people. But in Bahia de Kino, the local people were out cavorting in the heavy surf, something of a rarity in this protected bay. With Julieta under our belts, we're much less concerned than we might be — maybe much less than we should be.

On Monday morning, we took Cici in to the airport to catch her plane home. We've had a good week together. She's about to start classes at the John F. Kennedy School near her home in Oakland. We're glad she decided to take a break first. On the beach. With us.

But Cici is concerned about the coming hurricane. She jokes that Hurricane Cici is just leaving, as Hurricane Marty arrives. She's aware that her presence here is an intrusion into our very private lives. Yet it is an intrusion that we both welcomed. We weren't "just being nice" when we invited her. Not in Cici's case.

She encouraged us to consider staying at a hotel in Hermosillo until this thing blows over. We threw toothbrushes and a change of clothing into a "gringo bag," just in case. The people who live in the dilapidated shacks at Old Kino would think we were being more than a little foolish to leave, but what the heck.

We bought a paper at the airport and it showed Marty headed for the Sonoran coast south of Guaymas. We were expected to miss most of the wind in Kino but to get some welcome rain for the parched desert and the fields of irrigated crops. But there's really no way to predict the exact landfall of a hurricane.

From here, the rains will continue onward to the northeast, toward the US heartland. Hurricanes really are a remarkable "rain delivery system" for the entire continent. Presidente Fox was quoted in the paper as telling people facing floods from a different storm that, on the positive side, it filled the local reservoirs. I guess there's always a silver lining.

We put Cici on the plane, went to the store for a few items, and headed immediately back to Kino Bay before the rain turned a recent road detour into a quagmire. The detour is about two feet lower than the surrounding desert, so the road will probably be impassable for a while after it rains. Neither of us had seriously entertained the thought of staying in Hermosillo, anyway. We've each developed a fascination with this place, in all its moods.

On our way back to the coast, we spoke to a longtime resident who lives down the street. He said the latest report on cable TV said the storm would come ashore between San Carlos and Kino Bay on Tuesday afternoon. That's a lot closer to Kino than earlier reports estimated. He was getting out thick styrofoam panels to put beneath the storm shutters. We'll just lower the storm shutters and hope for the best, like we did the last time. We shall see if it's sufficient.

We enjoyed a fine meal with a decent wine from the wineries of Baja California, and we spent the evening working on a large jigsaw puzzle as the storm built outside. Heavy rain began falling and rattling against the windows. We heard a crash, which turned out to be a broom falling over outside and hitting the door. Later, we heard another crash, but nothing serious seemed to have happened so we ignored it. In the morning we found a shattered pottery sunface on the patio floor, blown from a nail on the wall to strike the door before hitting the concrete floor of the entry court.

The worst of the storm hit Kino Bay late Monday night. There was a definite increase in the windspeed outside the only window we left unshuttered. We awoke and listened carefully for a minute before returning to sleep. So far,

Epilogue

nothing important was breaking. The house had certainly weathered other hurricanes. If there were any large problems, we knew where our clothing was lying, and we'd dress quickly to deal with it. We're glad to be here again, on the shores of the Sea of Cortez.

Cici will undoubtedly look up weather reports for Kino Bay on the Web as soon as she gets back to Oakland. By now, she'll be very concerned about us. We'd like to send her a note: "Having a wonderful hurricane! Wish you were here!"

The people who live here seem to be very little concerned about the storm. We heard that one of the shrimp boats had engine problems and had to be abandoned during the storm, after the crew was taken off. The ship must have broken up out there, and that explains the large timbers and other pieces of wood we see in the heavy surf today. As for Kino Viejo, there seems to be little damage. It's a poor and simple town, mostly a collection of shanties, that sits in a low spot behind the dunes. Here the biggest issue is always flooding. Kids splash through the puddles in their bare feet like kids anywhere; most of the kids rarely wear shoes anyway. An unkind soul might say that in Kino Viejo, the wind just rearranged the debris. Yet its relaxed nature continues, with little apparent change. Its charming "No shoes, No shirt, No problem" attitude remains.

The sea birds are enjoying themselves in the high winds, especially those long-distance travelers, the frigate birds. They look like something out of an Edward Gorey cartoon as their jagged wings slice across the sky, like something straight out of "Mystery." Their wings barely move as they soar high overhead down the beach. They glide at an angle that loses just enough lift to stay airborne as they slip sideways across the wind. They make flight seem effortless — even in a hurricane.

All day Tuesday the storm continues. I drive to Restaurant Dorita in Kino Viejo for a newspaper to find out what's happening with the storm, but there are no papers today, at least not so far. Maybe in the afternoon. In the afternoon there are no papers, which is no surprise since the detour on the road to Hermosillo must be nothing but a mudhole by now. But it's not all that important, is it? We don't really need a newspaper just now. Life will go on without a newspaper.

On Wednesday, the morning dawns bright and clear, as if there had been no hurricane at all. The gentle sea returns, dark now with seaweed and shells ripped from the ocean floor to deposit on the beach. And filthy with the trash and detritus of human civilization. Cans and plastic bottles and pieces of heavy fishing rope mingle with the seaweed mass, as the sea gently and surely cleans herself of all this debris and leaves it at our doorstep. There are people on the beach scavenging for anything of value, but mostly it's of very little value. It's to our shame that plastic has such small value despite the fact that we fight wars for the raw materials to produce it.

So the sea cleanses herself, the people salvage a few usable items, and life returns to normal. The arrival, early each Fall, of these large *tormentas* is a normal part of life for Kino Bay. And that's really the point of all this, isn't it? That all this will go on without us, that life will continue long after we've all been called away. The best we can each hope for is that, in this brief moment made available to us here, we didn't just occupy space that could have been put to better use, that we somehow made this life a little better.

And Steve, I want to thank you for doing far more than your share to make life better for many other people in the brief time you spent here with us.

<blockquote>
I'll love you always,
Your brother, Perry
</blockquote>

Epilogue

Appendix

Alec, Steve, Janette, and Eliot. Spring 2001.

OBITUARY

Stephen Lloyd Wilkes, Janette Susan Carter Wilkes, and their youngest son, Eliot Carter Wilkes, of Albuquerque, were killed in the crash of a small plane in Beddel, Alaska, while vacationing there with friends.

Janette Carter Wilkes, born June 6, 1952, in Amarillo, Texas, was a distinguished physician, researcher, and Associate Professor in the Department of Internal Medicine. Janette grew up in Colorado and Idaho. She attended elementary school in Colorado, attended junior high school and graduated from high school in Buhl, Idaho, in 1970. She received her undergraduate degree from Linfield College in McMinnville, Oregon, in 1974 and the Doctor of Medicine degree from the University of New Mexico in 1978. She was a Pathology Fellow at UNM-SOM in Albuquerque from 1978 to 1979, a residency in Internal Medicine from 1979 to 1982 in Sacramento, CA, and her Chief Residency in Internal Medicine at UNM-SOM in Albuquerque. Janette received additional training at the New England Epidemiology Institute. She was board certified in Internal Medicine and held medical licensure in the State of New Mexico since 1986.Janette was the Director of the Diabetes Model Project and Area Diabetes Control Officer, General Physician, Public Health Service/Indian Health Service, Albuquerque Service Unit from 1983 to 1989. She was Assistant Professor, Veterans Affairs Medical Center and UNM-SOM, Department of Medicine, Primary Care Division, Albuquerque, from 1989 to 1999. At the time of her death, Janette held the position of Associate Professor with Tenure, Veterans Affairs Medical Center/UNM-SOM, Department of Medicine, Primary Care Division, and directed research in the Native American Diabetes Research Program, University of New Mexico. In 1972 Janette did independent study with Behrhorst Clinic in a small, rustic Indian village in Guatemala, working with rural populations to meet basic public health needs. This experience helped to form her deep commitment to addressing the needs of underserved and disadvantaged populations. Janette was the daughter of and is survived by Rosalie Carter of Albuquerque and LeRoy Carter, deceased. She is survived, also, by her eldest son, Alec Tomás Wilkes, 17, of Albuquerque.

Stephen Wilkes, born May 1, 1947, in Dayton, Ohio, moved to Albuquerque with his family in 1955. Steve attended elementary schools in Tipp City, Ohio,Sombra del Monte Elementary School in Albuquerque, Madison Junior High School, and Sandia High School, where he graduated in 1965. He received his Bachelors and Masters degrees in Education from the University of New Mexico. He began his early education career in California, then returned to Albuquerque to teach at Lincoln Middle School in Albuquerque. He served as Assistant Principal first at Alamosa Elementary School and Rio Rancho Elementary School, then as Principal of Comanche Elementary School and Chaparral Elementary School, all in Albuquerque.

Prior to forming Stephen L. Wilkes and Associates Management Consulting in 1991, Stephen managed organizations for seven years and served for three years as an internal management consultant to one of New Mexico's largest corporations. He was known internationally for his facilitation work with boards of major corporations, educational institutions, government agencies, and community organizations. Stephen is survived by his son, Alec Tomás; his mother, Alice Wilkes Matvichuk of Albuquerque; his father, Perry Robert Wilkes Jr. and wife, Bette Wilkes, of Albuquerque; one brother, Perry Robert Wilkes and wife, Carolyn Kinsman, of Albuquerque; three sisters: Elyse Wilkes Watson and husband, Jimmy Watson of Whortonsville, North Carolina; Nancy Wilkes Trujillo, her husband, Audon Trujillo, and daughter, Elyse Ana Trujillo, of Washington, DC; and Joan Wilkes Bockman, her husband, Kevin Bockman, and three sons Bo, Luke and Sam Bockman of Oceanside CA.

Eliot Carter Wilkes was born February 18, 1992, in Albuquerque, NM. He completed the third grade at Alamosa Elementary School and was active in both Little League and the Boy Scouts of America. Eliot was enthusiastically involved with learning piano and had attended Space Shuttle Camp in Alamogrodo, NM, for the last two years. Eliot is survived by his brother, Alec Tomás; his grandparents: Rosalie Carter, Alice Matvichuk, Perry R. Wilkes Jr. and his wife Bette, all of Albuquerque; his uncles Perry R. Wilkes, Jimmy Watson, Audón Trujillo, and Kevin Bockman; his aunts: Elyse Watson, Nancy Trujillo, Joan Bockman, and Carolyn Kinsman; and his loving dog, Kisses.

Stephen's father, Perry R. Wilkes, Jr., expresses that:

"It has been a great honor to have been the grandfather of Eliot C. Wilkes, the father-in-law of Janette Carter Wilkes and father of Stephen L. Wilkes. In their own ways, all three of these wonderful, adventurist, delightful, and dedicated individuals were warm and truly inspirational. Their involvement in the most challenging and meaningful things of life makes me think that, were they still with us, our future would be even brighter — much brighter.

"Without the presence of Eliot, Janette and Steve, I am moved to try harder to fulfill their dreams, as best I can do. Early on, it was Steve's efforts in helping to create the Rio Grande Bosque Nature Preserve Society that started me thinking about our tremendous resources and why they need protection and enhancement. Species diversity was the focus of his vision, and effort as a vital part of public education. The Rio Grande Nature Center was one result of this initiative."

Steve, Janette, Eliot, together with Alec, made their home in Albuquerque's North Valley in a community of loving neighbors and extended family, where they will be deeply missed, as they will be by countless friends and colleagues around the world.

A memorial service will be held at the Episcopal Cathedral of St. John, 3rd and Silver in Albuquerque; celebrant: Rev. Brian C. Taylor, Rector of St. Michael and All Angels Episcopal Church, where the family were long-time members.

In lieu of flowers, donations may be made to The American Diabetes Association, 525 San Pedro NE, Suite 101, Albuquerque, NM 87108; The Nature Conservancy, 4245 North Fairfax Drive, Suite 100, Arlington, VA 22203-1606; Doctors Without Borders, 6 East 39th Street, 8th floor, New York, NY 10016, or the Christian Children's Fund, Inc., 28221 Emerywood Parkway, Richmond, VA 23294-3725.

Albuquerque Journal, July 18, 2001

Duke City Couple, Son Die in Alaska Plane Crash

By Paul Logan
Journal Staff Writer

An Albuquerque physician, her nationally known consultant husband and their young son died Sunday when their sightseeing plane crashed into a mountain in Alaska.

Janette Carter, in her 40s, her husband, Steve Wilkes, 54, and Eliot Wilkes, 9, took off from a lake, but the single-engine floatplane lost power at about 500 feet. The wreckage was found about 180 miles northeast of Fairbanks.

Pilot Nancy Lewis, 48, of Fairbanks, also died in the accident.

St. Michael and All Angels Episcopal Church's parishioners were stunned by the loss, said the Rev. Brian Taylor, acting as a spokesman for the family.

"Everybody's on the phone with each other right now and everybody's in shock," Taylor said. "(The family) was greatly involved in the parish with youth programs and children's ministries."

Taylor had just returned Tuesday from visiting with the family's oldest, son, Alec, 17. He said Alec was devastated by the loss but "he's got an enormous amount of support of friends and family."

He called Carter "a remarkable" physician. She was an associate professor of internal medicine at the University of New Mexico, worked as a researcher in Native American diabetes programs and was on staff at the Veterans Affairs Medical Center, Taylor said.

"She was a real social-activist doctor, trying to do things for disadvantaged people with her medicine," he said.

See **PLANE** *on* **PAGE A6**

Plane Crash Kills Duke City Couple, Son

FAMILY PORTRAIT: Steve Wilkes, left, his wife, Janette Carter, and son, Eliot, 9, center front, died in a plane crash Sunday in Alaska. Another son, Alec, 17, center back, didn't make the trip.

COURTESY OF ST. MICHAEL AND ALL ANGELS CHURCH

from **PAGE A1**

Steve Wilkes was considered one of the nation's top retreat specialists and a talented management consultant, the minister said.

Wilkes worked with Fortune 500 companies and held retreats for presidents of Ivy League college organizations, Taylor said.

He was a former Albuquerque Public Schools teacher and principal. Taylor said Wilkes was so good at "doing group facilitation" at APS that Sandia National Laboratories hired him when it began an increased emphasis on civilian work.

Wilkes also was a member of the Watermelon Mountain Jug Band.

Funeral services are pending.

Other survivors include Wilkes' parents, Perry Robert Wilkes and Alice Matvichuk, and a brother, Perry Wilkes, and Carter's mother, Rosalie Carter. They all are from Albuquerque.

The Albuquerque Tribune, July 26, 2001

A great, generous man, Wilkes leaves behind knowledge and a big gap

I frequently have law students in my wills and trusts class practice will-drafting, using information from local celebrities. A few years ago, the wife of a symphony conductor volunteered. As we discussed the process, her husband said he thought he and his wife didn't need separate wills, because he hoped the family would die together and spare each other reciprocal grief.

Sherri Burr

I remembered that conversation last week after learning that Steven Wilkes had perished in a plane crash in Alaska with his wife, Dr. Janette Carter, and son, Elliot.

During the memorial services at St. John's Cathedral on Saturday, friends spoke of the humor and grace the family brought into so many lives.

I met Wilkes, a world-renowned facilitator, through the Albuquerque Arts Alliance. Although he routinely charged Fortune 500 corporations and Ivy League presidents thousands of dollars for his services, he donated his time to the alliance.

It's hard to believe that Wilkes is no more, and with someone as gifted as he was, it's sometimes difficult to find sufficient accolades. I offer, as a tribute, some of the techniques that made him so sought-after:

■ You never outgrow the need to do homework.

Prior to a retreat, Wilkes would canvass a group to gain a sense of the issues facing the organization. In his survey, he included the new kids on the block as well as the old-timers.

Wilkes called me about six months into my first term on the Arts Alliance board of directors to ask for my perceptions of the institution, in anticipation of an upcoming retreat. By the time we met for the retreat at a board member's home, he was able to present us with flow charts of the issues before us and a plan for the day's activities.

A former teacher and principal, Wilkes believed in doing his homework.

■ Introductions always help break the ice.

Wilkes began every retreat by asking us to introduce ourselves and speak of our recent artistic activities and/or vacation plans. We had no idea in June, when he mentioned his forthcoming vacation to Alaska, that it would be his last.

Those brief introductions provided us with insights into the current directions of other board members' lives. No matter how much members of a group thiank they know each other, there is always more to discover.

■ Write, write, write.

Wilkes used flip charts to record responses to issues, plans for the future, new committee assignments and so forth. His process seemed inherently democratic, because it was conducted out in the open. Even at Wilkes' memorial service, the rector announced there would be flip charts to record any feelings we wanted to share about the family.

■ Always conclude with a plan for action, accompanied by a timeline.

I have been to many retreats, and I believe this advice was one of Wilkes greatest gifts to those fortunate enough to participate in one of his. In so many secluded meetings, the group will have good discussions and then never change anything. After a Wilkes event, you departed feeling hope for the future of the organization, because the group had identified the problems and would now seek to resolve them in an accountable fashion.

Wilkes' death creates a hole in the Arts Alliance that will be difficult to fill. I sometimes felt that our gifts to him at the end of a retreat were inadequate, and yet he so graciously accepted each one. I am grateful to him for the time he so freely gave in his urbane and generous manner.

Perhaps the greatest testimonial to Wilkes and his family was the standing-room-only crowd that gathered for last Saturday's memorial service.

I don't know if Wilkes or his wife had ever expressed a wish to die together in their old age. Their untimely passing with their youngest son leaves behind a devastated eldest son and overlapping circles of grief-stricken family members, friends and colleagues.

From members of Elliot's Cub Scout troop to Janette's medical colleagues and Wilkes' enormous list of contacts, people squeezed into the doors of St. John's to pay their last respects to this individual who had touched an amazing number of lives.

The University of New Mexico Foundation is accepting donations to create the "Janette S. Carter, M.D., and Stephen L. Wilkes Memorial Endowed Faculty Development Series on Public Health and Community Service." For more information, contact Marnie Kern at the UNM School of Medicine at 272-5112 or "mkern@salud.unm.edu."

Burr is an Albuquerque writer and University of New Mexico law professor who is active in the state's arts community. Her column runs on Thursdays. Send e-mail to burr@law.unm.edu.

St. Anthony's Pharmacy Newsletter, 2002

Janette Carter, M.D.: *A Tribute*

Happy times. Steve Wilkes, Janette Carter, Teresa Balcomb and Jim Tryon outside their church three years ago.

Distinguished physician and researcher, social and community activist, outdoors-woman, daughter, wife, mother, friend, spiritual sister 1952 –2001

New Mexico
WOMAN
January 2002

St. Anthony's lost one of its original board members and long time dearest personal friend on July 15, 2001. Dr. Janette Carter, her husband Steve Wilkes and their youngest son, Eliot were killed in a small plane crash in the Alaskan wilderness while on vacation. The three are survived by their oldest son Alec and a devastated extended family.

Janette's passion for the healing profession of medicine began as a high school student when she spent 6 months working for Dr. Carroll Behrhorst in Chimaltenango, Guatemala with the Kaqchiquel Indians. Three decades later it was Dr. Carter, now a member of our board of St. Anthony's Pharmacy who convinced us to send $10,000 to support the Maternal and Neonatal Health Project designed by the Behrhorst Foundation in Guatemala. (See article on page 2)

Since it's inception in 1992 Janette and Steve have contributed thousands of dollars and much of their time to St. Anthony's. In May of 1997, Janette, Jim and Teresa traveled through the jungles of Nicaragua to do a site visit for a clinic St. Anthony's supports in Mulukuku. In a village with no running water and no electricity they spent an inspiring and life changing week together.

Janette completed medical school in 1978 then did a residency in internal medicine. She served as the Director of the Diabetes Model Project with the Indian Health Service. Her medical career was spent following her passion, the study of and the implementation of interventions that would prevent and treat diabetes in Native American populations. She wrote several grants that were funded by the National Institutes of Health which gave birth to The Native American Diabetes Project and "Sharing Wisdom": a primary prevention program for young Native American women with children living in urban areas".

On December 14, 2001, the Regents of the University of New Mexico presented a Meritorious Service Medal to Janette and a Recognition Medal to her husband Steve Wilkes.

The UNM School of Medicine established the Janette S. Carter and Stephen L. Wilkes Memorial Public Health and Community Service Lectureship to bring nationally and internationally recognized individuals to UNM to focus on community health issues of importance to New Mexico.

Janette was a deeply spiritual person. Her religion sustained and nourished her, giving her strength and courage to pursue her various passions. Her faith embraced all created things without exception, knowing that the divine assails us, penetrates and molds us. Her life was steeped in this rich knowledge.

Just before her death Janette went on a week's spiritual retreat in Belize. She wrote this simple prayer there one morning- words to live by:

Sacred being that blesses the morning.
That created all the four legged and two legged beings.
Remind me to live each day fully awake to the sacred within myself and all creatures.
That I might be blessed with glimpses of eternity as I move through the day.

Janette left St. Anthony's a wonderful legacy. We intend to carry on with her spirit, love and humor guiding us.

Yes! I want to help this man and others like him with a gift of medicine and essential health items in the coming year.

Enclosed is a donation of

$50_____ $100 _____ $150_____ Other _____

Enclosed is a pledge in the amount of $10.00 a month for one year to support St. Anthony's mission beginning _____.

NAME_____ ADDRESS_____
CITY_____ STATE_____ ZIP_____ PHONE_____
Email_____ FAX_____

A Life Passionately Lived

by Carolyn Kinsman

When word came from Anchorage last July that Janette Carter, her husband, Steve Wilkes, and their younger son, Eliot, 9, had been lost in the crash of a small plane in Alaska, it sent shock waves through a large extended family and a community that circles the globe.

How could someone in the prime of life — so vital, so competent, so engaged in serving others — be taken? There is no answer, but Janette's life offers important lessons for living.

Janette decided early on the medical profession and formed lasting friendships with others who shared her vision. As an adult, she regularly consulted, played, and collaborated with physicians around the world who had been friends in high school and college.

In 1972, while an undergraduate, Janette worked in a small Indian village in Guatemala to meet basic public health demands among rural populations. That experience changed her life, showing her both the need and the potential for medical service.

Janette Carter: Distinguished physician and researcher, social and community activist, outdoorswoman, daughter, wife, mother, friend, spiritual sister. (1952 – 2001)

After receiving her Doctor of Medicine degree from the University of New Mexico in 1978, completing residencies, and taking additional training in epidemiology, she was certified in Internal Medicine and licensed to practice in New Mexico. She then served for six years as Director of the Diabetes Model Project and Albuquerque's Area Diabetes Control Officer with the Public Health Service/Indian Health Service. Diabetes among Native American populations provided a strong focus for her future work, and in 1990 she founded the Native American Diabetes Project at UNM.

She built a staff of health professionals, researchers, and community workers, many of them Native American, to establish baselines, conduct basic research, and develop ways to bring about change. Her reputation for applied, not just academic, research spread throughout the medical community. Marla Pardilla, a co-worker, said: "When someone — anyone, anywhere — wants to know about diabetes research, the first person they call is Janette."

The team developed curricula and established educational programs on reservations, and the program grew. One weekend last year, the story goes, Janette took her staff to a hotel room and ordered out for food while they wrote a proposal for a new program to educate urban Indian women about preventing diabetes in their children. Recently, the National Institutes of Health awarded over $1 million to put this innovative program in place.

In recent years, as a representative of St. Anthony's Pharmacy (a New Mexico group of medical professionals providing supplies and pharmaceuticals to communities in need), Janette repeatedly made the rigorous trek to the mountain community of Mulukuku, Nicaragua, to work at the Maria Luisa Ortiz Women's Center clinic. The center, a cooperative formed by campesinas traumatized by the 1980s war and hurricane Jane, teaches self-sufficiency skills to women and provides health services to a community of 30,000.

How did she do it all? Janette was pulled — like many professional women — by conflicting demands: how to find time for children and her husband (an internationally-known consultant and facilitator who was often on the road), stay current in her field, fulfill her need to serve others, and take care of herself? Perhaps the explanation is that there were no separations in Janette's life; it was seamless. On the ski slope, in the classroom, at a patient's bedside, she was the same person.

She also had a special sense of humor and a free spirit. She was a formidable foe for Eliot on the basketball court, loved long-distance biking with her teenage son Alec, and cut a mean two-step on the dance floor. Once, while Janette was serving a residency in California, she and Steve decided to enter — just for fun — a country-western dance competition. They won first place in the state! Steve thought it probably had something to do with the fact that he was 6'5" and Janette, just 5'4". They didn't go unnoticed!

Janette was also deeply spiritual. She maintained a long-standing "spiritual sisterhood" with a small group of women in her church, St. Michael and All Angels Episcopal, and regularly took an annual retreat, often in Central America, to reexamine her mission and renew her spiritual commitment.

Greatly important was the love and support of her family. Janette's and Steve's partnership embraced every aspect of home and family; they made time to travel as a family and be actively involved with the boys' lives. Janette's mother, Rosalie, who was always available to help out when schedules were tight, now shares the family's North Valley home with their surviving son, Alec.

The July trip to Alaska was not just a vacation. Janette was introducing Steve and Eliot to some of the places she had been during a residency there — flying into remote Alaskan villages in the cold and dark of winter, where makeshift runways were lit by snowmobile headlights and breath froze instantly with every

Alec, Steve, Janette, and Eliot

exhale. But this trip was in summer, and when that little plane went down, it was after a day of hiking and picnicking next to a beautiful mountain lake, time spent with one of her long-time physician friends — and the pilot of the plane — a woman who shared Janette's passion for service and life.

The death of such a vibrant woman is difficult to reconcile. But there are no misgivings about Janette Carter's life. She lived it to the fullest — every minute of every day — and left for us a model of courage, compassion, excellence, and grace. **NMW**

***Carolyn Kinsman** is the designer of New Mexico WOMAN, and sister-in-law of the late Janette Carter.*

On December 14, 2001, the Regents of the University of New Mexico presented, posthumously, a Meritorious Service Medal to Janette Carter, M.D., and to Steve Wilkes, a Recognition Medal. UNM School of Medicine has established the Janette S. Carter and Stephen L. Wilkes Memorial Public Health and Community Service Lectureship to bring nationally and internationally recognized individuals to UNM to focus on community health issues of importance to New Mexico.

Nancy Lewis with her plane.

Fairbanks Daily News-Miner
Wednesday, July 18, 2001

Kin, friends recall full life of Nancy Lewis
By BETH IPSEN
Staff Writer

The doctor who piloted a floatplane that crashed about 50 miles south of Bettles Sunday was known as a safe pilot who would take friends on short sight-seeing trips to nearby lakes.

A friend of Nancy Lewis, 48, a retired Fairbanks family practitioner, called her very careful when it came to inspections and flying her 1977 Maule M-5.

"She was very focused," said Simon Rakower, a friend of about 15 years. Rakower, owner of All-Weather Sports, remembers Lewis coming into his shop and offering lunch-time plane rides to lakes in the Interior.

"She'd fly and land somewhere and look at the ducks and then go back," Rakower said.

This time, Lake Sithylemenkat was the lake of choice. But this time Lewis didn't come back.

She and three passengers from New Mexico, whose names haven't been released pending next of kin notification, died in the crash Sunday.

National Transportation Safety Board air safety investigator Clint Johnson picked through the wreckage of Lewis' plane located within a 100-foot-area about three miles from the lake Monday. It took only three hours to conduct an initial investigation, but Johnson said he hasn't determined the cause of the crash.
"Until we actually tear the engine down and totally disassemble the engine, it's all speculation," Johnson said from his Anchorage office Tuesday.

Lewis' husband of two years, Hugh Rose, said the recently retired doctor had about 1,000 flying hours. She had a long list of certifications, including commercial airplanes. She was qualified as a DC-3 co-pilot and was working on her pilot certification for Frontier Flying Service Inc. when her good friend, Charlie Adams, and first husband, Joe Finkel, died when the floatplane Adams was piloting crashed on a gravel bar in the Brooks Range in August 1996.

"That kind of derailed those plans," Rose said.

Rose and five of Lewis' close friends were at the couple's Yak Road log house Tuesday, fielding phone calls from friends and families around the country.

"I can't imagine how many people call her a friend," Robin Eagan said. Some she helped deliver into the world.

"She delivered many, many, many babies," Annie Caulfield said. "She delivered many of her friends' babies."
Rose said Lewis believed she had delivered close to 1,000 babies. She didn't have children of her own.

Lewis, a Long Island, N.Y., native, had retired in December after 20 years as a doctor in Fairbanks. She worked at the Northwind Family Clinic for 18 years and filled in for other doctors at the Fairbanks Clinic and Fairbanks Urgent Care Center.

What she had spent most of the last two years doing was traveling with Rose, a professional photographer and guide, and their dog, Jackson.

Rose was sorting through photos that he took of her on several of their trips, some of them as job assignments.

There was one of her in a biplane, Lady Katie, another of her on a back-country skiing trip in British Columbia. In each one, her smile was brighter than the yellow Arctic poppies that surrounded her in a picture taken near the Charley River.

Friends said Australia was the only continent Lewis did not touch. Her passion for travel was instilled in her from her parents, who joined her on many wildlife-viewing trips.

One of those trips was to Africa to view gorillas.

"She died at 48, but she lived 100 years," her father, Dick Lewis, said. Her parents arrived in Fairbanks from their home in Great Neck, N.Y., Tuesday night.

With Rose, there were two trips to Antarctica, one of those on which she worked as a ship doctor. Friends said Lewis wanted to eventually devote her time to caring for patients in remote locations and volunteering.

"We talked about going to Central America and doing a lot of things, but we hadn't made any concrete plans," Rose said.

Rose was guiding down in King Salmon when Alaska State Troopers notified him about the crash. A friend of his flew him out to the wreckage Monday.

He said the plane they owned was pretty well intact near a hill not far from the lake that was one of Lewis' favorite spots to take friends. The crater lake has a sandbar and a natural cliff surrounding it.

Her three passengers were visiting her from New Mexico. One of them was a fellow doctor who had gone to medical school with Lewis in Cleveland, Rose said.

Lewis herself came up here during a summer off in between medical residencies and hitchhiked across the state in 1974.

Then, in 1981, she moved to Fairbanks.

"She thought she'd try it for two years. After four weeks, she knew this was the place," Rose said.

During her 20 years in Alaska, she spent just about all of her free time in the outdoors, skiing, biking, hiking, fishing, kayaking or wildlife viewing, her friends said.

"She was an avid environmentalist," Caulfield said. "She had a lot of energy."

A memorial service will be held at 3 p.m. Saturday at the Dog Mushers' Hall on Farmers Loop.

© 1999-2001 MediaNews Group, Inc. and Fairbanks Publishing Company, Inc.

ALASKA PHOTOS
July 15, 2001

Nancy and Steve in the cockpit.

Lake Sithylemenkat

Nancy and Janette.

Eliot and Nancy picking blueberries.

Eliot leading the climb.

Eliot takes a cool dip.

Steve watches in disbelief.

Before heading back.

STEVE'S FLIPCHART

On Saturday, July 21, 2001, a Memorial Service was held for Steve, Janette, and Eliot at St. John's Cathedral in downtown Alburquerque. Father Brian, of St. Michael's and All Angels Episcopal Church conducted the service before a crowd that filled the building to overflowing. Steve Baca spoke eloquently of his long friendship with Steve, Dr. Tess Balcomb shared heart-felt memories of a long friendship with Janette, and Peter Dever told us of his special relationship with his "very good buddy, Eliot."

In recognition of Steve's years of work as a teacher, principal and facilitator, Maureen Baca arranged to have Steve's "flipchart" available at the reception after the service. Attendees were encouraged to respond to a simple question, written across the top of the page:

"How has Steve touched your life?"

- Steve introduced me to Jug Band Music in 1974. . . one of the best experiences of my life. – *Mouldy Lemon, aka, Mark*

- Steve taught me to "assess blame." – *Elizabeth "Betty"Szdley*

- You always made me laugh. – *Shelly*

- In every way. – *Cousin Gary*

- Thru Alice and my daughters. – *Ruth & Gene Frye*

- Every time I see a flip chart, I'll think of you, Steve. – *Brad Burns*

- May the rest of us love and grow into the void their absence has created. – *unsigned*

- I have my elevator praise all ready! – *HFH*

- Steve was a mentor to me – one of the wisest people I ever had the privilege to know. – *Nancy Uacher*

- Yes! With sparkle and sweetness. – *Ranya A. Fries*

- Thank you for the brief joyful moment of COOKIE DAY!
  – *unsigned*

- I'll never forget all those land meetings!
  – *unsigned (member of the 'land family')*

- Can we put this all in the parking lot? – *NV*

- A good walk on the ditch is best when you have friends to visit before you turn around and head back!
  – *Penny, Art, Eran & Keenon Vincent*

- I love his beautiful colorful sweaters. – *D. J. Rolls*
- The never-ending supply of cake, brownies & "orange steves." – *Allison Bean*
- His incredible enthusiasm for the children. – *Karen Smiles*
- Steve helped me get organized! – *Debby J.*
- Never knew what you could do with a kazoo! – *unsigned*
- At a VA retreat – a wonderful facilitator with high energy and humor. – *Mark Leo*
- As a new teacher, the support and encouragement I received from Steve helped me to know the importance of the job I was doing and gave me confidence that I was doing it well. Inspiration! – *Judy Scarbrough*
- We love to recall the days & years we lived across the street (Utah St) and Steve played with our kids. He loved to go fishing with me. We loved him. – *Mel & Esther Naus*
- Dear Steve, Thank you for helping me believe in myself. Your love and passion for life moved me forward in my own. Till we meet again. – *Hyacinth Sales*
- Steve was the "second Father" to our son, Micheal – always giving his words of wisdom, encouragement and wit – my memories will forever live with his warmth and caring for others! – *Anne McBrayer & Family*
- I've had trouble getting "my door" to open these last four years. Steve, your passing has brought a strong wind which has opened that door for me to go through with blessings. – *Angela W. Robbins*
- He used to put his hands on my head & his arm was so long I could only fight back up to his elbow! – *Little Sister Joan*
- What a wonderful mentor. I learned so much from Steve. He helped the Arts Alliance through many "slippery slopes." He will be deeply missed. – *Jan Hosea*
- His presence, his confidence in order out of chaos enriched our lives, empowered our community. – *Dede Feldman*
- Steve, You changed me forever. I will miss you more than I can imagine. I will try to use all you taught me. – *Maureen Baca*
- How has he not? Professionally and as a part of our faith community and as a friend. What a gift he and his family were to all of us. – *Kay Bratton*

- An inspiration to me of hope in organizational chaos – hope in humanity, thanks. Steve we will have to do our update in October on the other side. – *Steve Sprague*
- Steve told me that one day when he was walking down the hallway of a south valley school, a little first grader looked up at him and said, "a la you're so tall you could see into bird's nests!"
  – *George Winchell*
- Comanche Jug Band – we loved our fearless, innovative leader.
  – *Comanche teachers*
- He taught me inner peace & tolerance. – *Herb Koffler*
- Janette, I will always remember the wonderful birthday that we shared on the river. – *Kara Babb*
- Steve was present and he listened. He was completely generous with his gifts. He cared. – *Barbara Grothus*
- He was my mentor & my friend. – *Shirley Koffler*
- Steve asked Eliot "what book shall we read tonite?" (Bedtime when Eliot had just started Kindergarten.) Eliot thought a minute – "Well Dad, let's read the dictionary – I need to know more words."!!
  – *Charlotte Wagoner*
- Great hugs. (I'm 4' 101/2". He had to bend his whole body to reach).
  – *Deborah Hoffman*
- The positive energy flowing from him encouraged me when I was in a funk! – *unsigned*
- You couldn't take the smile off of Steve or Eliot.
  – *Love, Keenan Vincent*
- An inexhaustible store of love and kindness for everyone, and the willingness to cook me lunch whenever I came over. – *Evan*
- Our children were taught so well in a school led by Steve. We are so grateful for his leadership. – *Lewis & Barbara Barsky*

DE COLORES

De colores,
de colores se visten los campos en la primavera.
De Colores,
de colores son los pajaritos que vienen de afuera.
De colores,
de colores es el arco iris que vemos lucir.

Y por eso los grandes amores
de muchos colores me gustan a mí.
Y por eso los grandes amores
de muchos colores me gustan a mí.

Canta el gallo,
canta el gallo con el kiri, kiri, kiri, kiri, kiri.
La gallina,
la gallina con el cara, cara, cara, cara, cara.
Los pollitos,
los pollitos con el pío, pío, pío, pío, pí.

Y por eso los grandes amores
de muchos colores me gustan a mí.
Y por eso los grandes amores
de muchos colores me gustan a mí.

Canción folclórica española. From *Singing the Living Tradition*, 1993, Unitarian Universalist Association.

Steve often sang this song for family and friends and in performances with the Watermelon Mountain Jug Band.

NTSB Identification: ANC01FA084

Accident occurred Sunday, July 15, 2001 at Bettles, AK
Aircraft:Maule M-5-235C, registration: N9237E
Injuries: 4 Fatal.

HISTORY OF FLIGHT

On July 15, 2001, at an estimated time of 1530 Alaska daylight time, a float-equipped Maule M-5-235C airplane, N9237E, sustained substantial damage during a collision with mountainous terrain, about 50 miles south of Bettles, Alaska. The airplane was being operated as a visual flight rules (VFR) cross-country personal flight when the accident occurred. The airplane was registered to and operated by the pilot. The certificated commercial pilot, and the three passengers aboard, received fatal injuries. A VFR flight plan was filed. The flight originated from the Fairbanks International Airport Seaplane Base, Fairbanks, Alaska, about 0855, and was en route to Lake Sithylemenkat, located about 135 miles northwest of Fairbanks.

During a brief on-scene conversation with the National Transportation Safety Board investigator-in-charge on July 16, the accident pilot's husband related that the purpose of the flight was to show the three passengers aboard some Alaskan scenery. He added that the accident pilot frequently visited Lake Sithylemenkat to hike and pick blueberries.

According to personnel at the Federal Aviation Administration (FAA) Flight Service Station (FSS) at Fairbanks, the pilot obtained a weather briefing, and filed a flight plan with an anticipated return time of seven hours later. The accident pilot activated the flight plan at 0859.

About 1530, an emergency locator transmitter (ELT) signal was received by a search and rescue satellite, emanating from an area about 3 miles southeast of Lake Sithylemenkat. About 1600, a State of Alaska, Fish and Wildlife Protection Officer from Coldfoot, Alaska, aided by other aircraft in the area, began an aerial search in mountainous terrain near Lake Sithylemenkat. About 1800, the wreckage was located about 2,340 feet mean sea level (msl), in an area of mountainous terrain, and along the pilot's anticipated route of departure from Lake Sithylemenkat.

CREW INFORMATION

The pilot held a commercial pilot certificate with airplane single-engine land, airplane multiengine land, and airplane instrument ratings. She held an airplane single-engine sea rating. Her most recent second-class medical certificate was issued on December

5, 2000, and contained the limitation that corrective lenses be worn while exercising the privileges of her airman certificate.

A review of the accident pilot's personal flight records revealed that her total aeronautical experience consisted of about 642.8 hours, of which about 13 were accrued in the previous 6 months. The flight records also revealed that the accident pilot had satisfactorily completed a biennial flight review (BFR) on July 11, four days before the accident.

AIRCRAFT INFORMATION

The airplane had accumulated a total time in service of about 1,207.0 hours. Examination of the maintenance records revealed that the most recent annual inspection of the airframe and engine was accomplished on December 8, 2000, about 27.0 service hours before the accident. Further examination of airframe maintenance records revealed that between September 1999, and March 2000, the accident airplane underwent an extensive airframe overhaul and repair process, about 72.0 service hours before the accident.

The engine had accrued a total time of about 1,207.0 service hours. The maintenance records note that a major engine overhaul was accomplished on March 10, 1992, about 659.0 service hours before the accident.

METEOROLOGICAL INFORMATION

The closest official weather observation station is Bettles, which is located about 50 nautical miles north of the accident site. At 1552, an Aviation Routine Weather Report (METAR) was reporting in part: Wind, 110 degrees (true) at 9 knots; visibility, 10 statute miles; clouds and sky condition, 6,000 feet scattered; temperature, 75 degrees F; dew point, 51 degrees F; altimeter, 29.95 inHg.

The State of Alaska, Fish and Wildlife Protection Officer that was involved in the search for the accident airplane, reported that after locating the wreckage about 1800, he landed his wheel-equipped Piper PA-18 Super Cub along a ridgeline, located about 1,000 feet above the wreckage site. He said that during the approach for landing, he encountered winds out of the southeast, estimated to be 17 to 20 knots. He added that the location of the accident airplane's wreckage was situated on the downwind side of the mountainous terrain. The mountain ridgeline is oriented about northeast-southwest.

COMMUNICATIONS

After the accident flight departed Fairbanks, the accident pilot activated her VFR flight plan. There were no reports of additional communications with the accident airplane.

WRECKAGE AND IMPACT INFORMATION

The National Transportation Safety Board investigator-in-charge, accompanied by two FAA inspectors from the Fairbanks Flight Standards District Office, examined the airplane wreckage at the accident site on July 16, 2001. The airplane was located in an area of mountainous terrain, at an elevation of about 2,340 feet msl, within a "U" shaped valley. The surrounding peaks ranged between 3,000 to 4,000 feet msl. The southwest end of the valley slopes downhill, towards areas of lower, flat terrain.

All of the airplane's major components were found at the main wreckage area. The main wreckage debris path was oriented on a 300 degree heading, and downhill. The nose of the airplane came to rest oriented on a 120 degree heading. (All headings/bearings noted in this report are magnetic).

Postaccident investigation revealed that the nose of the airplane impacted the soft, tundra-covered terrain. The airplane came to rest inverted, with the tail of the airplane positioned downhill of the 15 degree slope, in relation to the main wreckage area.

About 12 feet uphill from the main wreckage site were three impact craters. The two outer most craters measured about 3 feet in diameter, 6 inches deep. About 9 feet uphill from the main wreckage site, the center crater measured about 6 feet by 3 feet, and 13 inches deep.

A 3-inch deep depression was visible in the ground, extending horizontally in front of the three craters. The depression extends from the tip of the left wing, to the tip of the right wing. Both outboard halves of the wings had spanwise leading edge aft crushing with more crushing along the lower portion of the leading edge. Both lift struts remained attached to their respective wing and lower attach points.

The propeller hub remained attached to the engine crankshaft. The three propeller blades were loose in the propeller hub. One propeller blade was almost straight, but displayed slight torsional twisting, and slight aft bending. The second propeller blade displayed about 20 degrees aft bending about 6 inches inboard from the propeller tip, and slight torsional twisting. The third propeller blade displayed about 5 degrees aft bending about 4 inches inboard from the propeller tip, with slight torsional twisting.

The engine cowling, fuselage firewall, and the instrument panel were crushed and displaced aft. The engine was partially buried in the soft, tundra-covered terrain. The engine sustained extensive impact damage to the underside, and lower front portion. The carburetor assembly was broken free from the mounting plate. An internal examination of the carburetor bowl contents revealed about 10 cc of clean, uncontaminated fuel. The fuel sample collected from the carburetor bowl tested negative when subjected to water detecting paste.

The firewall mounted, glass, gascolator bowl was found intact and was completely full of clean, uncontaminated fuel. The fuel sample collected from the firewall mounted gascolator tested negative when subjected to water detecting paste. The gascolator screen was free of contaminants.

Flight control system cable continuity was established from each control surface to the cabin/cockpit area.

The floats were torn from their respective fuselage attach points. The forward nose compartment of each float assembly was crushed aft, and buckled upward.

The main/cockpit cabin area of the fuselage was extensively crushed and distorted. The primary crush zones extended from the firewall area back to about the forward doorpost, and encompassed the pilot and front seat passenger area. The fuselage was buckled and folded, and the empennage was positioned downhill.

The vertical stabilizer, horizontal stabilizer, rudder, elevator, and fuselage, aft of the cabin area, had minor wrinkling, and buckling. The flight control surfaces remained connected to their respective attach points.

The main fuel selector valve was selected to the LEFT fuel tank setting.

On August 9, 2001, an engine examination and disassembly was conducted at Chena Marina Air Service, Inc., in Fairbanks. No preimpact mechanical anomalies were noted during the examination of the engine, or engine accessories.

MEDICAL AND PATHOLOGICAL INFORMATION

A postmortem examination of the pilot was conducted under the authority of the Alaska State Medical Examiner, 4500 South Boniface Parkway, Anchorage, Alaska, on July 17, 2001. The cause of death for the pilot was attributed to multiple blunt force impact.

A toxicological examination was conducted by the FAA's Civil Aeromedical Institute (CAMI) on August 24, 2001, and was negative for any alcohol or drugs.

WRECKAGE RELEASE

The National Transportation Safety Board released the airframe and engine wreckage to the pilot's husband on August 9, at Chena Marina Air Service, Inc., in Fairbanks. The Safety Board retained no components.

A FAMILY HISTORY
for Alec

Alec,

I think I should tell you some things about our family, now that your Father is gone. It seems to me that's one of the things an uncle is supposed to do, to pass on a more or less accurate accounting of the family's story.

There's much more to tell than I can put into this book, mostly concerning people who went work each day and left no monuments to their memory. I'm sorry I don't know more about them, but they are also part of the very modest recent history of our family.

The important thing is for me now, is to tell a few personal stories about my brother, your Dad. I'll try to do that here.

But before we get into those memories you should also know that, buried deep in your past, there were some famous people who you are related to. Some were even infamous and nefarious rogues whose exploits inspired the writing of a few decent books. I have some of these volumes on my bookshelf, and I'll be happy to share them with you.

Some of these books contain the story of an ancient relative named John Wilkes (no relation to John Wilkes Booth, who was named after John Wilkes, a famous American actor you may also be related to), a well-known London journalist in the 1700s. I believe he was also Lord Mayor of London at one time. He was booted out of Parliament several times, at the personal direction of King George III, and was described by Hogarth as "... capable of a degree of abuse, for which licentious is too mild a word." He was a source of great amusement for some, and an unfortunate distraction for a mentally unstable King at the time England was losing the American Colonies.

There are a few books about Admiral Charles Wilkes of the US Navy. He's the man who discovered and named Antarctica — really, it's true. Wilkes drew the first accurate maps of most of the islands of the South Pacific when he commanded a major expedition there. Many of those maps are still used today. He was also twice court-martialed for his arrogance and insubordination, and so his very important accomplishments are little remembered today.

And then there's Captain Perry Wilkes, a Union Officer who was awarded a Congressional Medal of Honor for bravery in battle on the Red River in Texas during the Civil War. He went on to become a highly-respected Steamboat Pilot on the Ohio River. According to newspaper reports of the time, his funeral was a major event in the river town of Louisville, Kentucky, where he now lies buried in Cave Hill Cemetery near the grave of the famous explorer, George Rogers Clark. He's also not far from the grave of Colonel Sanders. Much of history is like that, a marriage of ironies, of the important with the ridiculous.

Your Great Grandfather, Perry R. Wilkes, was President of the Gateway Distributing Company, the wholesale dealer in Louisville, for Old Fitzgerald, Early Times, and other brands of Kentucky Bourbon Whiskey. He was also, as he proudly told us now and then, "the youngest President, ever" of the Kilwinning Masonic Lodge in Louisville.

Your Great Grandmother, Flossie Mae James, had polio as a child and had to wear custom-made prosthetic shoes all of her adult life. Polio was a common disease when she was young, and our generation was very lucky to have escaped it, thanks to the development of the Salk vaccine. For this vaccine alone, Dr. Salk was considered to be a major hero of our time..I still remember how strangely shaped Grandma's shoes were, and how much difficulty she had walking.

Grandma told us she was related to Jessie James, but I don't know the details. She and her sister, Aunt Lou, were very proud of that ancestry since Jessie James was considered by many as a mythic folk hero who robbed the corporate bosses and often helped the poor, although our Grandpa Wilkes didn't want to talk about it. There was some speculation that she played the piano in saloons and dancehalls before she married our Grandpa, but he didn't want to talk about that either. Still, somebody has to be related to Jessie James and it might as well be us, it might as well be you.

Your relatives on the Rosenberger side of the family were not as flamboyant as the Wilkeses, so there don't appear to have been books written about them. However, they were probably better regarded by their peers for their quiet attention to the duties of hearth and home. There's a legend about a German princess and a valuable necklace that was always passed down to the youngest daughter, but our family missed it by one daughter a long time ago. That's the kind of legend every family has, and it may not be true. On the other hand, I used to dismiss our Grandpa Wilkes' stories about John Wilkes in London, until I had an English History class in college and found out he was right.

As for the Carter side of your family, you'll have to ask your Grandmother Rosalie. Your mother was an intelligent and remarkable person, and I'm sure there's a story or two worth telling about the Carter family.

I don't know what other tidbits may be buried in the dusty archives of history. But that will have to wait for another occasion, for the investment of more research, for the gift of time for the writing. That may happen at some point in the near future, but it can't happen now. If I never get around to it, there are plenty of well-written books about these fellows on the shelves already.

With ancient history acknowledged and put away, we can proceed. What follows is just the story of a family with four young kids who headed west on a great adventure. It's a simple story of how we came to settle in the desert southwest, where we were joined by our youngest sister. I won't tell every detail of everything we did, since much of it would be uninteresting. I won't dwell on things that might be hurtful to people, but I won't shy away from them if it's important. Thankfully, there's not much that was hurtful about Steve's life. He was a remarkable person.

Here's what I remember of the story:

My younger brother Steve was born on May 1, 1947. We were born less than two years apart. Steve was christened Stephen Lloyd Wilkes, after St. Stephen, an early Pope who was stoned to death in Rome during the persecutions of the Emperor Valerian, according to sources I read as a kid. Steve's middle name, Lloyd, came from Mom's only brother Lloyd Rosenberger, our Uncle Buddy. Buddy was named for Prime Minister David Lloyd George of England, who our Grandfather Jacob Rosenberger held in high regard for his peacemaking efforts at the end of the First World War.

Our Grandfather Rosenberger – everybody called him "Pop" – had a great interest in peacemaking, natural history, and anthropology. He was a religious skeptic who went to the Unitarian Church because they held interesting lectures on the archaeology and the natural world of the Ohio River Valley. He was always curious about the environment and the animals that inhabit it. I remember him showing me drawers filled with arrowheads, spear points, and the like that he had collected over the years while hiking near the River.

Pop, who was of German heritage as is all of our family on that side, was skeptical of the intense anti-German propaganda of the Second World War because he remembered similar campaigns of intentional falsehoods during the First World War. Unfortunately, after the War he was shocked to realize that much of the information about the Jewish extermination camps was true. I think Steve got much of his interest in peacemaking and mediation from Pop.

Steve and I shared most of the same friends and the same adolescent culture. We shared the music that formed our lives and many of our ideals; the music often served as an anthem, a soundtrack, for our entire generation.

We always shared the same bedroom. We each wanted a room of our own, but that was never possible in a large family of modest means. As the family grew in means, it also grew in size; and we had to make do. That's just how it was. Girls get their own rooms; boys live in the barracks. I suppose it has a leavening effect on society. Lycurgus of Sparta would have understood.

Because we were so close in age, I probably knew your father better than anyone. I knew him as he navigated the troubles and mischief of youth. Later, he attained the wisdom and maturity of those who survive the dangers of childhood to enter manhood, and assume the heavy mantle of family and social responsibility. Somehow we both survived, with very few scars to show for it.

My earliest memories are of the two of us sharing the first of many bedrooms in a little white clapboard house in a family housing area on Wright-Patterson Army Air Corps Base located near Dayton, Ohio. Our father, your Grandfather, had been a Lieutenant in the Army Air Corps at the end of the Second World War, but he served his time and became a civilian employee. Ours was a simple home that looked just like all the others on the block — that's how the military prefers it. The two of us played in a sand box in the front yard with other neighbor kids. It wasn't very long before we were in a sand fight, for which I got the blame because I was the oldest. And, truth to tell, I probably did start the fight. I usually came out on top in those days because I was bigger than Steve, at least until he started growing faster than me.

It wasn't long before we moved off the military base, to a little house in the country. It had something to do with a certain incident that involved our father putting up a nice little white picket fence across the front of the yard to keep Steve and me out of the street. It was a well-built fence that looked really nice. And it sure made our house stand out, since we were the only ones on the block — and maybe even on the entire Base — with a little white fence in front. Unfortunately, the military brass does not appreciate anyone with a flash of individuality — they don't call military clothing "uniforms" for nothing. Very soon, orders arrived from Base Headquarters that the fence must go.

Dad decided to fight for his little white picket fence. I don't really remember much about it, and I'm sure Steve didn't either since we were both preschoolers at the time. And I don't know how long Dad was able to hold out before the full weight of the US Army Air Corps prevailed. But the fence was taken down. And very soon after that, we were living way out in the country where a fellow could put up a damn fence if he wanted to, and no stuffed shirt General could tell him he couldn't.

What I mostly know about the incident I read many years later when Mom, your Grandmother Alice, showed me a faded clipping of an article that appeared in the Base newspaper. There was a headline reading something like, "Wilkes Loses Fence War," and there was a big picture of our Dad looking very unhappy as he pulled his nice little fence apart. But looking back now at that day long ago, I'm proud to say I don't believe that incident ever deterred your Grandfather from charging into battle against equally hopeless odds at any point in the future. And maybe that's where Steve and I were first inspired to fight for an ideal, if we knew we were right. Even if we might be a bit uncomfortable in the process.

So we left the military base, and suddenly we were country kids, living along a highway outside a little town with the odd name of Tipp City, Ohio. It was probably every young boy's dream to live out in the rural countryside where there were creeks and meadows filled with frogs, snakes, mice, turtles, and every other critter we could imagine. I remember it as a very happy time.

Regarding the odd name of our new little town, the story goes that two small towns in Ohio had named themselves after the famous battle of Tippecanoe. Don't ask me what the battle was famous for, since I was only a kid when we lived there and I don't know much about Ohio history. It had something to do with President William Henry Harrison, I think. Well, somebody researched the issue and found that the other town had the name first. The battle was still important enough that our small town settled on the strange name of Tipp City. Your Grandfather used to call the local baseball team, TCU, the Tipp City Underdogs. He's always been witty, your Grandfather.

Steve and I slept in bunk beds in the same room. At first, I slept on the top bunk because I was older and less afraid of the height. I seem to remember that we took turns for a while, but that I was moved to the top bunk permanently because I couldn't resist kicking Steve's bunk from the bottom after I was sure he had just drifted off to sleep; younger brothers are a wonderful thing to annoy, aren't they? Eventually, our parents figured a way to squeeze both beds into the room side by side and life continued more peacefully for awhile.

Until The Great Chewing Gum Incident, that is.

There was a popular song in the 1950s that went, "Does your chewing gum lose its flavor on the bedpost overnight?" I don't know why Steve was always interested in collecting gross things; but now that we each had a separate bed, and he had bedposts of his own, he decided to construct a massive chewing gum wad on one of them, a mouthful at a time. It was mostly intended as a practical joke on our mother, and we waited to see how big it would get before she noticed it residing there. It ended up quite large, and multicolored from all the different flavors he had slapped on top. I remember that it looked like some kind of alien brain, all lumpy and disfigured. Mom was making the bed one evening as Steve and I stood there with expectant grins. Finally she worked her way nearer to the head of the bed. Then she turned to look for a pillow case or something and stopped for a second to register this deformity glued to the bedpost. Suffice it to say she thought it was considerably less humorous than we did, and neither of us ever did that again.

We loved being country kids with creeks to explore, full of minnows, crawdads, garter snakes and tadpoles. Just behind our house there was an old abandoned section of the Miami and Erie Canal, but there was no water in it. There were some very poor families living in "picturesque" shacks down at the end of the lane that ran beside our house — families that threw all their trash into a big pile just outside the rickety front door; it was a big interesting pile. Steve and I rooted through the pile and found some corn cobs that the hogs had finished with. Then we grabbed some sticks, and made ourselves a couple of semi-functional-looking corn cob pipes. We thought we looked real cool "smoking" on those pipes. When we showed up back at the house with handmade corn cob pipes in our mouths, your Grandmother screamed and whisked them away from us. After she found out where we had gotten those disgusting things, she forbade us from ever going back to the end of the lane again. She also didn't approve of the smutty comic books we borrowed from a kid who lived in one of the shacks. It didn't seem neighborly to us, but we weren't going to argue with Mom about it.

We were soon distracted by other things that were within easy bike-riding distance. There was a place down at the creek where a big old grapevine hung from a huge tree, and we spent a lot of time there pretending to be Tarzan, swinging across the creek to the other side. When we didn't quite catch our footing on the far bank, the grapevine swung back to the middle of the creek and stopped. There was nothing to do but drop off into the creek and crawl through muddy water to the bank. I don't remember if we were ever banned from the grapevine, but that could have happened.

There was a big beautiful pond in an open area behind some nice stone houses just a ways down the highway that ran in front of our house toward the town of Troy, Ohio. Someone had built this pond out of colorful flat stones laid in mortar, and they really looked beautiful with the water lapping against them. I stopped there one day and laid down to look over the side into the clear water for bluegills that might be lurking in the shadows far below. Maybe one would dart out to grab a grasshopper that landed on the pond. I watched water striders on the surface, minnows in the shallows, and various little bugs scurrying through the bottom mud as I lay there, feeling a bit drowsy, on a warm and lazy summer afternoon. Then I saw a movement and I noticed a beautifully colored shape that looked like a brilliant piece of rope on a ledge just a couple of layers below me. It blended into the rocks so well that I hadn't even noticed it, until it moved and pulled itself back into the shade. Suddenly I remembered a picture I saw in a magazine, and I realized it was a copperhead, sunning himself just about six inches below me. I leapt to my feet and ran home as fast as I could, looking over my shoulder now and then to make sure he wasn't chasing me. I told Steve about the snake, and neither of us ever went anywhere near that pond again.

I remember the two of us playing beside the narrow highway in front of our house, watching cars as they appeared like distorted visions out of the shimmering heat of summer, and studying the bubbles of tar that rose up in the broiling sun. We'd find sticks to pop bubbles in between the very few cars that traveled the highway, back in those days. And we'd usually end up with some interesting tar patterns on our clothes for our Mother to comment about when we went into the house. Having the time to study tar bubbles on a blistering highway was one of the gifts of an endless Midwestern summer.

A few miles down that country highway, in the direction of town, there was a man who raised baby rabbits, chickens and ducks. His last name was Corey, I think. There isn't much of anything that's cuter to a couple of young boys than a baby rabbit or a baby duck, even a baby chicken. The man raised them for food, mostly, and he slaughtered them when they were big enough for market. Some of the rabbit's feet he made into lucky charms like you used to see for sale now and then. He was kind enough to send each of us home with the bloody "raw materials" to make our own lucky rabbit's foot charms. When we got home with those bloody rabbit's feet we learned about another one of our Mom's peculiarities.

On another visit to the rabbits and ducks, he gave me a little duckling of my own. She was a beautiful little duck who "adopted" me as her parent, and she followed me everywhere. When I took her to school on the bus one day for "Show and Tell," the teacher told me I wasn't supposed to bring animals and I had to take her home. This wasn't possible since we lived so far out in the country. So she had me take my little duck to the Principal's office to get permission. I took her out into the hallway and I set her on the floor. Then she followed me, quacking all the way, to the office. As we rounded the corner, the ladies in the office melted at the sight of the two of us, and sent us on in to see the Principal. He was very amused when I set her on his desk and quickly gave me permission, before some "accident" occurred on his important papers. Steve, Elyse, and Nancy all loved that little duck too, and they helped me feed her. She grew up into a fine duck and enjoyed living on our little rural farmstead.

In the mid-1950s we got a used 1949 Ford Sedan that Dad drove to work each day. I don't know what we had before that, probably a Model T, or something. He also used the Ford as a truck by removing the back seat. He took Steve and me with him whenever he went to the dump to scavenge some bricks or other materials for one of the sheds and other projects he was always building. He was forever restless.

Steve and I helped pick out used bricks and load them in the car. Back at the house, we tossed them onto a big pile for later use. In our spare time we'd clean off the mortar and stack them neatly, although we both would rather have been off somewhere playing with our friends. The two of us did not constitute a committed work force. We also learned to take nails out of salvaged boards and straighten them to be reused. These are rare skills today in a land where waste seems to be a virtue, and I'm glad we learned them. I have actually used these skills at various times in my life.

There was a family who lived in a shack at the dump. The dump generally smelled awful, and there was always a fire burning up something that made it smell even worse. I didn't know how those people could live like that. The man of the house scavenged through the debris each day and hauled the best stuff to one side where he made a living reselling it. He always had a few interesting toys and trinkets that he had found. Dad would sometimes buy us a used toy from the dump guy just to keep his work crew more or less happy.

A kid named Maxie lived next door to our house, just beyond a fenced acre of grass that we owned along the road. Steve and I shared a lot of adventures with Maxie. We spent our time playing at his house and in that big field filled with tall grass. We'd squash down the grass in a small area and hide there from our mothers and our little sisters. We ended up just covered with chigger bites every time we did that; but it was a great place to hide out when you wanted to, or maybe even needed to.

Dad got the idea that we could raise sheep on that acre of grass to supplement the family income. Dad was always looking for some way to make a little extra money for the family, and this was his latest idea. Two of our sisters, Elyse and Nancy, had arrived by then, and I'm sure a little extra income was a good idea. He pulled the back seat out of the old 1949 Ford, and Steve and I went with him to get some sheep from a farmer he knew. As I recall, we put a bunch of straw and hay in the back so the sheep wouldn't stumble around and hurt themselves when we drove home. Steve and I rode in the back to calm the sheep, as Dad drove slowly over the least-used backroads he could find. Dad built a "stile" — a kind of ladder affair — over the fence so the animals couldn't get out, but we could. And then, for a short time, we were in the sheep business.

Soon after we got the sheep, our Uncle Dick, who lived in Indiana near Louisville, gave me a young billy goat. Uncle Dick was a Colonel in the Army, and he raised goats and horses at his farm in his spare time. That's probably where Dad got the idea for the sheep. A young billy goat is about worthless to a farmer if he already has one male goat to keep his female goats happy. A young billy doesn't give any milk, and he just ends up fighting with the head goat. They're usually sold off for meat. This young fellow's days were numbered, until Uncle Dick gave him to me.

I was overjoyed at the idea of owning a small goat and, to show my gratitude, I even named him Uncle Dick after my uncle. That seemed to amuse all the aunts and uncles and older cousins considerably, and I was glad to see them all so happy. Steve and I spent a lot of time playing around, pushing and tussling, with that cute little goat named Uncle Dick, until he got to be a big strong goat, with big strong horns. Our friend Maxie never really seemed to be able to relax around Uncle Dick, and the goat knew it. A goat can sense these things and this one always seemed to butt a little harder when he played with Maxie.

One day Steve, Elyse, Nancy, and I got the call to come in for lunch. Maxie's mom had called him in earlier, so he finished sooner than we did. We were eating our sandwiches and looking out the window toward that grassy field, when we saw Maxie step out his back door. He came down the back steps, and walked over to our front gate to climb into the field. Uncle Dick was grazing at the far end of the field. As Maxie stepped down onto the grass, Uncle Dick looked up and started to watch him very intently. Maxie tried to stay calm as he walked in the direction of the stile, but he looked nervously over and saw Uncle Dick staring at him. When Maxie was about halfway across the field, Uncle Dick stopped chewing and took a step in his direction. That's when Maxie bolted for the stile.

Uncle Dick was quite a ways out there in the field, and Maxie had a good head start on him, but a goat can be very fast. He streaked after Maxie, and the two of them arrived at the stile about the same time. Maxie just had time to bolt up the first step or two and had gotten close to the top when Uncle Dick aimed for his butt and saved him the trouble of scaling the rest. All four of us kids sat there at the table with our sandwiches poised in mid-bite, as we watched Maxie come sailing over the fence and out into the yard. After that day, Maxie never took the shortcut to our house again.

Those were good days, as I remember it. Very good summer days, and almost endless, with much to keep a couple of curious young boys fully occupied. There were times, of course, when dense banks of heavy rain clouds drifted south from the Great Lakes and blotted out the sun for days at a time. On those sodden boring days we raced each other on roller skates around that steel center pole in the basement. I think every home in the Midwest back in those days had a center pole in the basement, and kids spent hours down there on rainy days racing around it.

We also spent a lot of time down in the basement during the long, gray months of winter. I remember entire months when it was too cold, wet, and miserable to spend much time outside. Mom would dress us up to go out in the snow for a while, but we got cold very quickly and headed back to the house. There were entire months when we didn't see the sun. That's when we learned to play games together — games like Chinese Checkers and Monopoly — and to assemble jigsaw puzzles and model airplane kits. I don't remember having a television in those days, but I remember Monopoly games that were almost endless, and there was always a jigsaw puzzle in progress on a side table somewhere.

But mostly I remember the warm and endless days of summer.

We went to see Lake Erie one summer. We drove to Sandusky and took a ferry boat out to the island called Put In Bay. It was a windy day, the passage was rough, and very soon, all the kids were sicker than we'd ever been in our lives.

The cabin was full of hot sweaty, smelly people, and some of them were even smoking. Steve and I went out onto the bow of the boat, and waited for spray to cool us down. That, and the fresh cool air, seemed to help. We were all relieved when the boat docked at the island. The trip had taken hours.

We walked around for a while and looked at some interesting things, but mostly we were all dreading the ride back to the mainland. None of us wanted to take the boat back, but there didn't seem to be any other way. Finally, someone mentioned there was an airfield on the island, so we went to check on the cost. They wanted some outrageous amount, like maybe $50 dollars, to fly the six of us back. Dad swallowed hard and coughed up the money, and we boarded an old Ford Trimotor aircraft. It was an ungainly looking craft that pilots called The Tin Goose, but it had a reputation for reliability. We were glad that it had three engines, in case one or two konked out.

The old plane coughed into life, roared down the runway, and lifted into the sky. She flew high over turbulent Lake Erie far below, and got us safely and quickly back to the mainland. Steve and I were very excited about flying in this old plane. In those days not many of our friends had ever flown in a plane of any kind, and we'd have some stories to tell. Even today, it's a rare person who can claim to have flown in a Ford Trimotor, although they were common at one time. I think our Dad was even a little stoked about it, despite his grousing about the cost and about a bunch of complaining kids. He'd been fascinated by aircraft since he was a teenager. He even had an aerobatics endorsement on his Pilot's License from 1944, although he didn't tell me that until the late 1990s.

We were born in those heady days of American power after the Second World War, and the events of those days clouded much of our lives. I remember someone pointing into the sky one day at a Mig jet that banked over the countryside near our house. It was captured during the Korean War, and they were doing tests on it at Wright-Patterson, to understand Russian weapons if we ever went to war with them. To a kid growing up in the fifties, war with the Russians seemed to be inevitable — and due to the development of nuclear weapons, we knew it would likely be the last war in human history.

There was always talk of war in those days, in Korea, in the Suez, always somewhere — and there was the constant threat of instant annihilation in a nuclear war if any world leader decided to press the button. We had nightmares about it — kids like us and the other kids we knew. We talked about it now and then, Steve and I. We each decided there wasn't much we could do about it, so we mostly ignored the possibility and went on with our lives. But I know it affected the way we saw the world.

One day Mom said we were moving to New Mexico.

"Mexico?" we asked. "We're going to Mexico?"

"No, NEW Mexico." She repeated the name more clearly.

We four kids stood there and looked puzzled. Mom got out a big map of the United States. She pointed to where we lived in Ohio. Then she drew a line with her finger almost all the way across the country to the state of New Mexico. And then she pointed to a place called Albuquerque.

"We've been transferred to Albuquerque." she explained. We were moving to another town with a funny name. We were used to it by now.

Dad had been in and out of the Army Air Corps and now he had joined the new US Air Force. As an aeronautical engineer, it was the logical choice for him; and he joined as a Captain. Now we were being transferred. All four kids looked puzzled again.

"What's 'transferred'?" was our next question.

Steve and I had watched a lot of western movies. We were excited at the prospect of heading west where there were real cowboys. Maybe we'd even be cowboys ourselves someday. According to the map, this town with the funny name was real close to Santa Fe. Any kid who'd seen a few westerns knew that Santa Fe was way out there in the very heart of the Old West.

Our sisters were a lot less excited than we were, and they didn't want to leave their friends behind. But we were leaving, like it or not, because we'd just been "transferred" and we'd better get used to it.

It was September of 1955 when we headed west. We planned to stop in Louisville to visit the family before the long drive, and we needed to arrive in Alburquerque before school began. Dad built a fold-up plywood platform to fit just behind the front seat of the 1949 Ford sedan that would carry us to our new home. The platform stayed in the trunk with our bags until we kids got tired of sitting and watching endless barns and cornfields go by the window. When we got sufficiently tired and wanted to lie down or we just wanted to sit around a game together, Dad would stop the car and unfold the platform into that space behind the seat. Mom would cover it with a blanket or two and some pillows to turn the entire back seat area into a big cushioned bin, and we would lay down for a game or a nap.

This most often occurred when our parents got tired of all the noise four kids could generate and they thought it was about time for us to take a nap. And with me the oldest at ten, Steve at eight, Elyse at six, and Nancy just four years old, peace and quiet was rare during the five or six days it took us to make our way west in those days before Interstate Highways. Nap time was mandatory as we made our way across a vast country and down the main street of every little town along the way.

In pre-Interstate days, the highways of the nation wound their way from one small town to another, and there were stop signs and stoplights that had to be obeyed in each one of those towns. If we were lucky, there might be a stretch of straight highway through open farmland for maybe ten miles before the speed limit signs told us to slow down for the next little town. Each one of these towns seemed to have its own unique character in those days, with interesting stores along a very busy main street filled with shoppers. And each town seemed to have one or two unique and beautiful buildings that set it apart from all the rest. Looking back on it now, I can remember the feeling that I was getting a glimpse into the life of each one of those little towns, and every time the car slowed down Steve, Elyse, Nancy, and I crawled to the windows and watched wide-eyed as we drove down yet another pretty street in yet another pretty little town.

I thought that some day when I had lots of time, and enough money, I would make the trip again, and I'd stop at all those wonderful looking little cafes in those interesting downtowns we passed along the way. I'd take another look at all those wonderful and interesting buildings that defined each little town. But within a shockingly short time, all that was gone, as the Interstate System sucked the economic life out of small town America.

Incidentally, the concept of seatbelts, and kiddy car-seats, was unknown in those days. We just curled up on the back seat together under a blanket, and nobody in those days seemed to realize that it could be a very dangerous thing to do.

We stopped to visit the relatives in Louisville. It was likely to be the last time we would see them for a few years because the distances were so great, travel was expensive, and cars were not very reliable. This was a major move back in those days. There were tears among the womenfolk as our visit came to an end and we climbed back into the '49 Ford to head west. There were always a lot of tears shed among the women whenever anyone in our family left to go anywhere. Steve and I flashed that knowing smirk of little boys everywhere trying to appear wise and unaffected beyond our years.

After leaving St. Louis, we were on Route 66, the famous two-lane highway that linked the country together all the way west through the hills and grasslands of Oklahoma and Texas, and beyond. It was a very long trip for a car full of kids and no air conditioning. We welcomed those few moments when the road took us down into the cool air beside a creek or river, but those times became fewer as we got further west.

Eventually we arrived at the New Mexico state line. At this point the land fell off into grass-covered mesas and distant mountains. It was clear that we had finally arrived in The West, but there were no cowboys to be seen. There hadn't been any in Oklahoma or Texas either, which were surprisingly flat and green and didn't look much like The West at all. We wouldn't see a cowboy until we went to the State Fair a few weeks after our arrival. Still, there were tall mountains looming mysteriously in the distance as we got closer to Alburquerque, and we kids began to wonder how our little car was going to get over the top of them. The problem resolved itself when the road wound through Tijeras Canyon, and into the broad Rio Grande valley on the other side.

We snaked through the rugged rocky canyon with huge boulders perched high on each hillside, until Route 66 rounded one last bend and emerged hugging the side of the mountain. Before us lay the entire desert valley of the famous Rio Grande, river of song and legend. It was a sweeping panorama I will never forget, and one for which four Midwest kids were entirely unprepared. We had never seen anything like this before. And neither had our parents.

We suddenly left the mountains behind and followed the highway onward for many miles through a desolate landscape as we passed a few shabby outlying buildings standing alone in the desert. When we reached the gateway into Sandia Army Base, the guard waved us through with a salute, since our Dad was a Captain now. We were placed in temporary accommodations — kids and all — at the Bachelor Officers' Quarters, called the BOQ. It was a cramped apartment for all of us, but it had a swimming pool. Unfortunately the water was cold, even in the heat of summer, because of the dry desert air. Within a week or so, we moved to a small home in the Wherry housing area on base as we waited for our new tract house on the mesa to be built.

The first order of business for a couple of young boys was to explore the new and strange environment we now called home. We quickly discovered horned toads and lizards, since they were everywhere There were so many that we used to take them for granted. Yet in years to come we'd realize the devastating impact domestic cats and dogs have on small animals who are unprepared for these new, and well-fed, predators who kill for sport.

Soon we shared a converted single-car garage in one of those suburban homes that were creeping out across the landscape surrounding every major city after the War. From the end of our block, there was nothing to the north until you got to Santa Fe. All my stuff and Steve's — our books, our treasures, and our uncompleted projects — lay intermingled again on shelves, in closets, and on the floor.

Steve began to assemble a collection of miniature liquor bottles over the next few years of exploring the mesas and alleyways near our home. None of the bottles had been rinsed, and they retained most of the dirt that had embraced them where they were cast away. Some contained a small measure of magical brown liquid, and we could open them to get a whiff of the distilled delights that awaited us someday as we grew slowly into manhood.

Steve kept his precious collection safely out of sight beneath the bed, but that day arrived when Mom decided it was time for major housecleaning. She was less than pleased to discover Steve's "filthy" (her colorful description) treasures beneath the bed. His work of many years was immediately dumped into the trash, and he never regained the creative drive to rebuild it.

We went to an elementary school that was about a mile away, across the mesa. We rode our bikes there and back each day. One day, as we were sitting in class, a huge flock of sheep engulfed the school. An old shepherd and his dogs were driving them across the open grasslands toward the mountains. We all jumped from our seats and ran to the windows to watch the chaos of this sea of wool as they moved away from the building, in a noise of bleating and barking, into the distance. During our rides onto the mesa, we sometimes found old sheep skeletons that were left behind.

Steve once found some huge 50 caliber machine gun bullets someone had pitched beside a dirt road. We could see that they were live rounds and we handled them carefully. We gave them to the police who thought that was a very interesting find, since each was like a small bomb.

We spent our days, when we weren't in school, exploring the vast open lands that stretched from the end of our block far to the north. We caught bull snakes, gopher snakes, hog-nosed snakes, leopard lizards, collared lizards, ground squirrels, and even a rattler once. We kept them in a pair of cages that our Dad built nestled into the ground in our backyard. One Saturday morning we were privileged to watch a large horned toad give live birth to more than twenty young. She deposited each glistening sack on the ground to dry in the sun. When the sack burst, a tiny horned toad blinked its way into the world, fully formed and very hungry. The cage was crawling with baby horned toads for a few days, until we took them far out onto the mesa and let them go.

We weren't allowed to watch much television; and frankly, most of it was not worth watching. Most of it still isn't worth watching. The exceptions were Friday night, if we'd been good, and Sunday night when the entire family might watch Disneyland, or Sid Caesar, or Ed Sullivan. In those days, Disneyland was considered "educational television."

On Friday night, we sometimes got a soda pop and a TV dinner, and we parked ourselves in the den to watch adventure shows until we fell asleep. The family had a set of those metal folding TV tray tables and each of us had one for our food and our drink.

Steve discovered that if you shake your soda pop with a thumb over the top, the fizz builds up and you can shoot it into your mouth. He decided that if a little fizz is a good thing, then a lot of it is even better. So he clamped his thumb tightly over the top and shook the bottle for a while longer than he should have.

Soon he felt the pressure building beyond his ability to control it. He looked at me with a panicked expression as he realized the mess he was about to make as soda sprayed all over the room, and the trouble he was going to be in. Our parents were in the living room talking with friends when the pressure pushed Steve's thumb off the top of the bottle and a tower of brown soda shot all the way to the ceiling. He sat there stunned for a moment as the mess dribbled back unto him, and then he hurried to clean things up as best he could. We all helped out, as we fell over ourselves laughing.

The conversation in the living room kept our folks distracted long enough to clean things up, and for soda to stop drifting from the ceiling. I happened to be in the den a few days later when Dad noticed a large brown stain on the ceiling and wondered what it was. I looked at the stain and shrugged my shoulders as I left the room. I heard him muttering something about a roof leak as I wandered out the back door. That large brown spot stayed on the den ceiling for years.

Later on, we spent Sunday nights at Luther League, the youth group at St. Luke's Lutheran Church. Each kid brought a can of soup to make dinner with. Girls always wanted to put the similar kinds of soup together in separate pots so that everything looked nice. But sometimes, the boys would dump it all together into a very tasty, but disgusting, grey mess.

Steve was often the instigator of this.

There were usually candles on the tables in the youth hall so it looked like a nice evening meal. Steve found that if you dripped warm wax from different-colored candles onto the back of your hand, your hand would soon look like it belonged to "The Mummy." After his hand was fully covered, he'd slide it under some poor girl's nose like he was reaching for the salt. Girls would always let out a gratifying scream. He also discovered if you drip hot wax onto the top of a glass of KoolAid, you could seal it in. Then when you "accidently" knocked the glass over onto the table, people would leap from their chairs to avoid the "spill." Red KoolAid worked best because it was so visible.

About every other summer, we'd take a long road trip back to Louisville. When we arrived, the aunts would "divvy" us up and we'd spend a week here, a week there, until we'd seen all our cousins. On one trip back to visit, I think it was our first since moving west, we went through Nashville to see our Kippes cousins. From there we headed north up the "Dixie Highway" through the verdant landscape of Kentucky, to Louisville. Steve was very young when we left the Midwest and he didn't remember how green everything was. As he looked out the window and watched the endless green landscape go by he asked, "Who waters all that grass?" He never lived that one down.

In his teens Steve was drawn to music, and it would be an important part of his life for the next thirty years. He enjoyed singing in the Church Choir, and he had a much better voice that mine. He also cared more about it than I did.

Some friends of his started a band called The Puritans, and they did a mean version of "Not your steppin' stone." They became pretty well known, locally. Steve became their "Personal Manager," and he booked them at gigs all over town. Later they changed the name to The Chöb, after our cousin Dennis Kestler said it meant "zit." To a bunch of teenage boys, grossing people out always carried a high premium. I remember Dicky Hanson, Quintin Miller, and Keith Bradshaw were in the band, but I don't recall the others.

Of course, Steve was best known for being with The Watermelon Mountain Jug Band. It all began with those jug band parties he held at the modest apartment he rented for several years in the one hundred block of Columbia Street southeast. Steve would invite friends from college, and from his job as a hospital orderly, to come for a kind of sing-along evening gathering. He provided an assortment of large glass jugs, spoons, washboards and other "instruments," and everybody just played along to LP records of Jim Kweskin and the Jug Band. It didn't really matter if you were off-tune or not, as long as you made sufficient noise and had a good time. Steve drank his beer out of a bedpan he borrowed from the hospital, and that would usually gross out a few people.

As I recall the story, Steve met Jeff Burroughs and a few others at a Community College class on Jug Band music. Jeff, Steve, Barbara Piper, Gary Oleson and Mark Zimmer were the original members of the Watermelon Mountain Jug Band. Steve was always quick to say that Jeff was one of the few legitimate musicians in the band, along with Ben Perea who later took Mark's place. The rest were teachers, in real life. Joanne Sartorius joined the band later to help out with the singing, and others have sat in now and then.

They had a good run while it lasted. And it lasted long enough to celebrate their Tenth Anniversary at the historic Kimo Theater, one of the city's architectural treasures that they helped to save. At the party, Mayor Harry Kinney read a Proclamation designating the alley behind the theater as Jug Band Alley, and a sign hung there for several years, until it was stolen.

Steve told many stories about the Jug Band, Alec, and you should probably ask Gary Oleson, Barbara Piper, or Ben Perea to tell you about it if you're a stickler for detail. On the other hand, you might ask Jeff Burroughs, if you're up for a good yarn. Meanwhile I'll tell one incident, and hope I get it mostly right.

The Band decided to see if they had what it took to be an actual professional group. It would be a break from teaching, and it might pay pretty well, if they could pull it off. They had already been on national TV, on the same program as some guy in a skimpy costume who could tear a phone book in half. With those kinds of credentials, they decided to go for it. They went to Las Vegas and had a number of adventures that Gary and Jeff would be better at telling you. But they got a gig on the road, in Wendover, Nevada, to see if they liked playing every night in bars and casinos. It was a test of their commitment.

They played for about a week in this god-forsaken outpost on the Nevada-Utah line. Steve told me there was about nothing in every direction except the Bonneville Salt Flats, and a few distant mountains. The only reason for this place to be there was that it was the closest place for people from Salt Lake City to gamble.

They played each night, paired with a couple of dragged-out, road-weary guys, called the Off Hour Rockers. After their weeklong gig finally ended, all five band members huddled to discuss whether they wanted to spend one more night in the motel and leave early in the morning. The unanimous vote was to leave immediately and never look back. They realized they weren't cut out for life on the road.

Steve told these stories with his wonderful wry wit, and he always saw the humor in every situation. I know he was a little sad they weren't destined to be famous musicians, but I think he was satisfied with the fame they'd achieved around Alburquerque. He liked that old Roger Miller song, "Kansas City Star," about the modest aspirations of a guy who's famous in one town, and who's happy with it. I think he could relate to that.

I happened to be driving past La Mesa Community Center and Park just the other day, and I remembered it was once the site of the Tesuque Drive-In Theater. We were just young gringo kids back then, freshly arrived in a new and strange land, with no idea how to pronounce Tesuque. It was "Tess — uh — kyou" until we learned more about our new home. Then it became "Tess — oo — kay," and the rich languages of the Rio Grande valley became part of our lives, part of us.

As we learned more about this fascinating culture we'd cringe when local TV newsmen, mostly retread used car salesmen, butchered Spanish and native words on television in front of thousands of people. Were they willfully ignorant? Had they no pride? Where did they get these guys anyway? It was always guys, and with the most ridiculous pompadours. We were only kids back then, but were we expected to take this crap seriously? Dick Knipfing was the first one able to pronounce the names, the first one who treated the Spanish language with dignity.

The thoughts go on so many tangents. There's so much to say, so much to tell.

I stopped to talk with the contractor adding a gym to the Community Center and we reminisced about the old Tesuque Theater. I recalled summer nights in our teenage years, just out cruising, maybe catching a movie.

"We'd go in with two guys in the front seat." I said. "And four in the trunk."

The contractor laughed and remembered. He and his buddies had done the same.

I remember Jesse Layton and me in the front seat of my 1953 Buick Super V8 two-door sedan with those mellow twin exhaust pipes. Those twin glass-pack mufflers made a nice smooth rumble as I drove down the street. The inside was red and black rolled naugahyde. That car was a beauty that cost me $300, a lot of money on my salary as an after-school fry cook at $1.25 per hour. Steve was in the trunk with, I think, Rick Stravasnick, Skip Johnson, and Steve Precker. We had to leave the spare tire at home and fit Steve in first because he was so tall. He laid on his back and his head hung over into the spare tire well.

After we closed the trunk, Jesse chucked and whispered, "Let's go find a rough road first, before we go to the movie!"

It sounded like a great idea.

We drove off toward the mountains and found a fairly rough road, just for laughs. The guys in the trunk started yelling and wondering what the hell was going on. They knew there was no dirt road between our house and the Drive-in. We yelled back that we ran into an unexpected detour, but they knew better. The only explanation was that they were now at our mercy and had been screwed.

We finally got to the theater and yelled for them to be quiet as we passed the ticket seller. We found a good place to watch, and we let everybody out of the trunk. We mostly spent the night making wisecracks while some mindless teenage movie played on the screen ahead. People in the other cars glared at us because they had paid full fare, and because we were making noise. But none of us really cared about that. We were young and callow with a whole wide world ahead of us.

It was a good time to be alive.

In the summer of 1963, when I turned 18 years old, Steve and I, our sister Nancy, and our cousin Gary Kirk, headed east to visit the relatives in Kentucky. It was August when we drove off in my 1953 Buick Super, and we enjoyed the mellow sound of those twin glasspack mufflers all the way across the country. I had joined the Marines and was to report for duty in September, so this would be my last stretch of freedom for a while. We drove non-stop, on the freeways when we could, on the old highways when we had to, and we made it in 24 hours.

We were exhausted.

It was hot when we arrived, the "dog days" of summer; and we spent as much time as possible swimming in the pools, rivers, lakes, and quarries that are found all over Kentucky and southern Indiana. We were all a bit older, and things had changed. Some of the older cousins were now married, some were in college — things were just different. But we had a wonderful time together.

As our month came to an end, some of the male cousins decided to throw me a rolling farewell party. Looking back now, it's not the sort of thing I'd recommend, but it happened nevertheless. We took my car and we bought a couple of cases of beer to stash in the trunk. Gary drove, I was in the passenger seat, Ronnie Kippes, Dennis Kestler, and his friend George were in the back seat. We passed bottles of cold beer around. Gary stayed sober. As one of the younger cousins, Steve was not included in this caper.

We spent the night driving around Louisville drinking beer and looking for interesting things to do. We stopped at a girls slumber party that Dennis knew about, but they asked us to leave before their parents found us there. Gary saw a girl he knew at a drive-in; and I whispered, "Ask her if she has a gullible friend." Gary looked at me in disbelief.

Sometime after midnight we dropped off Ronnie and George and returned to Dennis's house, exhausted and sick. We each crawled into our beds and dreaded the arrival of morning, when Steve, Nancy, and I had to drive back to New Mexico. I couldn't face breakfast, but Grandma Wilkes had planned to feed us a big lunch before our departure. Steve looked at me like I'd committed the crime of the century. I told him not to tell anybody what had happened, and he and Nancy and I went to eat at Grandma and Grandpa's place.

After we left, Steve did most of the driving while I laid on the back seat and moaned. I was thankful then for his well-developed sense of responsibility and his careful driving. He drove us safely onward to the west, toward our home, until I recovered enough to help out.

Steve later joined the Air National Guard and went to boot camp near San Antonio, Texas. He was amused that his Recruiting Officer was Sergeant Albert Sanchez, better known by his stage name as Al Hurricane y los Nightrockers. You couldn't listen to a hit radio station in the 1960s without hearing a promo for one of his events at the Civic Auditorium.

The military life didn't suit Steve any better than it did me, but he tolerated it better. He even bought a short hair wig to wear to monthly drills so he wouldn't have to look like a buzz-cut idiot the rest of the time. It was the late 1960s, and short hair was way out of fashion. After a weekend drill near the end of his enlistment, a Sergeant waved to him as they were leaving. On an impulse, Steve reached up and pulled off the wig, and his bushy Afro sprang to life. The Sergeant's jaw dropped as Steve hopped into his lime-green VW van and drove away. It was a small victory for individuality.

I bought a house after my military stint. Actually, I bought a shack. It was over on the west side of town, in a very poor neighborhood, at 467 61st St. NW. The street had only recently been claimed from the sandhills. It cost me $4500, which seemed like lot of money in those days.

Steve drove our mother over to take a look at it, and when Mom saw it, she cried. She couldn't believe one of her sons was going to live in such an awful place. Her family history had been one of hard work to make life better for the next generation. This looked like the worst kind of backsliding to her. Steve shook his head in silent disbelief at my latest folly.

What I saw in the place was a solid core structure with a few shoddy additions constructed by Charlie Espinosa, the next door neighbor who had owned it. The "sewing room" addition was nothing more than old wooden pallets and cardboard with a coat of paint over it. I only spent about three hours demolishing it and hauling it all to the dump. There was another addition which had been an old shed, until Charlie dragged it over to the side of the house and nailed the two together. I put a foundation under it, insulated it, and paid Fecho Chavez to add a very pretty little corner fireplace. I put in new kitchen cabinets, built a new bedroom with a nice brick floor at the back, replaced all the decrepit windows, rewired the place, and restuccoed it. Early in the process I stopped keeping track of the hours I put into this project, as there was no way I'd "make wages" — even 1960s wages — on this one. Anyway, it was better than watching TV.

While I was working, I noticed that most of the yard was higher than the house and I planned to do something about it when I got the time. But a heavy thunderstorm intervened. As the lightning crashed, I ducked inside to watch the first big raindrops hit the ground and be absorbed by the sand. But the surface quickly became saturated, and large rivers of water began flowing toward the house. I stuffed an old shirt and a few other things under the door as a dam, but it was hopeless. The rain kept falling and the water kept coming, until there was about a foot of water in the house. For a while, I just stood there in the mess and laughed. After the rain stopped, I dug a big hole outside the back door so the water could drain outside. I immediately began to build a low retaining wall at each door to stop the flooding, with a landscaped sunken entry court to absorb excess rainfall.

After many months of hard work, I finished the house. It was almost completely new and bore no resemblance to the old shack. It had a charming pueblo style, and looked pretty good. Even Steve thought so. When I got divorced and needed to sell the place a few years later, he bought it from me, for $14,300.

Within a very few years, he married Janette. They loved living next to Charlie, a good friend and a source of endless amusement. They lived there for many years, until Alec joined the family. As Alec grew, they began to realize they would need a larger home.

Janette had always liked horses and wanted to live where they did, or at least nearby. They had their eye on a very nice lot in the North Valley, and they asked me to design a home for them. We spent most of a year working on a design, then the owner of the lot decided not to sell. This was a terrible blow, especially to Janette. She'd had such strong visions of living there that nothing else seemed acceptable.

I dropped by their home on a Saturday morning to discuss our next move. I had recently designed a home for another couple in an intriguing part of the far North Valley. These people and others had a vision to create a sense of community through design. Each homesite shared ownership of some common areas, and the homes were required to be solar heated. I thought this new community had the potential to fulfill most of their ideals. I thought it could be the right place for Steve, Janette, and Alec, and I suggested we go look at it.

Janette was too discouraged to even consider it, and we dropped the idea.

Then I said something like, "I can really understand your disappointment, after all that hard work. Say, you know it's a really nice day. Why don't we just go for a nice drive and do a little, oh, sightseeing?"

Steve immediately caught my drift, and saw the twinkle in my eye. He knew me well after all those years of sharing a bedroom together. He grinned and asked, "You mean like, maybe, take a little, uh, drive in the, uh, North Valley?"

"Well now, there's an idea. I hadn't thought of that," I said. Steve and I could be almost as good as a cut-rate Vaudeville team at times. "Come to think of it, there are some nice little roads out there. Be kinda nice to get out of the house for a drive, doncha think? Maybe even smell a little country air."

"Maybe even see some horses." Steve added.

Janette looked at the two of us with a grudging grin. Our transparent shenanigans could be almost too much at times. But she recognized that we really wanted to cheer her up, and she was willing to go along with the joke. We headed out into the North Valley, and "accidentally" turned down the lane leading to the property I had described. We crossed a bridge over a tree-lined irrigation ditch and drove past a field of alfalfa. There were horses grazing in the adjacent field, and there were vestiges of an old orchard at the back of the property. Janette immediately saw the beauty of this site, with its stunning views of cottonwood bosque to the west and mountains to the east.

We soon began drawing plans for their new home. They, and their children, became important contributors to this new community and helped it grow as a family. The Land Family became its semi-official name. This is where they would live for the rest of their lives.

As with any project, an excellent design requires an excellent client. Steve and I shared a common aesthetic vision. We hadn't spoken of it before, but for each of us, one of our most memorable influences while studying at the University of New Mexico had been the beautiful older buildings designed by John Gaw Meem. Especially the west wing of Zimmerman Library and the Alumni Chapel. Steve and Janette couldn't afford to build on such a massive scale, so we discussed the elements of the design. Then we worked to recreate those proportions and details on a more modest scale. We spent months reworking the design until we had it right.

I still consider it the best home I've ever drawn.

There is still much to discuss in the lives of Steve, Janette, and Eliot, but every detail of a person's existence should not be reducible to a single volume. They deserve better than that. There will be more to write another day.

There are other people with memories as valuable as mine, and I'd hope they'll invest the time to record them. For me, it's been a very good thing to do. It could be good for others.

But it is right that I have come to an end. I believe this is a good place for me to stop.

Family members gather with some of Eliot's classmates in front of the plaque placed in Eliot's classroom at Alameda Elementary School. Back row: Uncle Perry and brother Alec. Second row: Cousin Rachel, Aunt Carolyn, Grandmother Alice, Grandfather Perry, Grandmother Bette, and Grandmother Rosalie. Front: A few of Eliot's classmates.

From Steve's bookshelf.

Postscript

ALEC TOMÁS CARTER-WILKES
(July 13, 1984 – July 9, 2018; not quite 34 years of age)

My nephew Alec was a bright young man, impulsive, artistic, creative, conflicted – and for me, forever an enigma. I think that may have been our common fate because we were, in so many ways, so similar. He was forever flailing at the strictures and conventions of the era he was born into. I understand that. I was the same in my early years.

But I was not thrust into a conflicted situation at the early age of sixteen, a sudden 'trust funder' living off the estate of deceased parents. That can be a heavy emotional burden, with legal 'gatekeepers' guarding the young heir from his family, for better or for worse. At any rate, an artificial distance was created, and he and I never really had a chance to discuss all of this. And he never had the important opportunity to share with his aunts and uncles the simple realities, troubles, and frustrations of life that most of us have to deal with every day.

Alec receded from the family, as I had done in my own late teens and early twenties. I considered that to be normal behavior as he struggled to find his own space, try new adventures, and make his own mistakes, without the counsel of parents and family. But as he grew older Alec became even more estranged behind the walls he had erected, often keeping his location a secret to his family and all but a few of his friends. I tried to make contact in our visits to Albuquerque but was usually unable to find him. And the few times we had together were too brief to be of consequence. I decided that was his choice and not to push my way into his world, hoping he would emerge on his own as he matured. But over the years, we grew to know each other less and less.

Now I mostly remember Alec as a sensitive young man growing up in the verdant valley of the Rio Grande, and I recall the pain he felt each autumn when the ditch bosses cut off the flow of water into the old *acequias* that provide life to the fields. That's when thousands of fish are left stranded each year in rapidly emptying puddles and the waiting birds enjoy their yearly feast on the helpless victims. Alec and his dad would gather buckets of flailing and panicked fish, and take them to the river to be released to swim freely once again. Alec could never save all the fish stranded in those miles of emptying ditches, but he did what he could. And that's just one example of the inner pain he felt each day.

Alec surely inherited a weight of guilt from being the only survivor in his family and little of the stabilizing influence of his aunts and uncles. He was instead surrounded by his age cohort, young punk-rockers filled with their own teen anguish and little real life experience.

I dropped by Alec's messy crash pad one day (it was not unlike my own at that age), and was met with the glaring eyes of various young hangers-on. In their view I was not the young revolutionary I used to be, but was now part of an older oppressor generation who knew nothing of consequence that might interest them. I did my best to ignore them, although the idea of delivering a good smack across the face did occur. I thought, "You haven't earned the right yet to be so damn smug," – although I had the same cheap smirk at that age.

I was there to give Alec a used copy of *The Big Sky* (1947) by AB Guthrie Jr, the classic adventures of a young man in the Old West that left an impression on me many years ago. Alec had built rock walls with a friend in Colorado and enjoyed the outdoors, so I felt he could relate to this tale of a mountain man in the bitter winters of pre-Civil War Montana trekking south to the tiny village of Taos. Alec took a quick look at the book, said thanks, and tossed it onto a pile of debris in a corner of his living room. I was stunned at this treatment of a piece of literature, but tried to accept it as the flip way of youth these days. I never heard about it again, or whether he even read the book.

Soon, he was covered in grisly tattoos and playing head-banger rock with a heavy metal band. He sported an odd side-cut hairdo and worked as a bouncer in a downtown bar. He became ever harder to reach and still did not share his address. And then, he killed himself.

Ironically, Steve had told me a few years before his own death in Alaska, "We're just going to enjoy Alec as long as we can, as he crashes his way through the world." Or words to that effect. Steve and Janette, and even young Eliot, had recognized early on that life would be a constant struggle for Alec and that he might not live to an old age.

I don't know whether to regard Alec's birth on Friday the 13th as a harbinger of sorts. And 1984, the year of his birth, has long had special meaning as the title of George Orwell's dystopian novel. Had he heard Albert King's blues version of "Born Under a Bad Sign"? I really don't know how to deal with all of that and I don't recall him ever mentioning the peculiar circumstance of his birthday. But did that weigh somehow on his final decision?

So where does the fault lie here? – if fault can be assessed at all. Was there a turning point that was ignored, or misunderstood, a place where an intervention could have made a real difference? Could someone have done something, anything, to alter the tragic outcome of Alec's short life?

While that's probably unknowable, it remains a question that haunts me and others. Was there any way to penetrate the wall he built around himself? And did we try hard enough to find a way through it? What is unclear in the clutter, the noise, of everyday life, sometimes becomes clear much later.

In the end, the world—at least Alec's corner of it—was too much for him, and he took his life at an early age. It's a sad ending, a tragic bookend of sorts, to the once-promising story of my brother's entire gifted family.

So for all my failures at really knowing Alec—at actually finding the essence in his life's tragic and fraught trajectory—I will forever be sorry. And his memory will be with me forever.

Although our time together was too brief, Alec, it was my good luck, my challenge, and my great pleasure, to know you.

Perry Robert Wilkes
April 2021
Bahia de Kino
Sonora, MX

www.ingramcontent.com/pod-product-compliance
Lightning Source LLC
Chambersburg PA
CBHW081228080526
44587CB00022B/3861